Political
LONDON

First published 2007
by Historical Publications Ltd
32 Ellington Street, London N7 8PL
(Tel: 020 7607 1628)

© **Richard Tames 2007**

ISBN 978-1-905286-18-8
British Library Cataloguing-in-Publication Data
A catalogue record for this book is available from the British Library

Typeset by Historical Publications Ltd
Reproduction by Tintern Graphics
Printed in Zaragoza, Spain by Edelvives

The Illustrations

The following kindly gave permission to reproduce illustrations:
London Borough of Camden, Local Studies & Archives: *51*
Fabian Society: *74, 86*
Metropolitan Police: *70*
Richard Tames: *1, 7, 9, 17, 23, 31, 39, 92, 98, 105, 108, 123, 124, 125, 126, 128, 138, 139*
City of Westminster Archives: *134*
Other illustrations were supplied by the Publisher

The front jacket is a coloured etching by James Gillray, 1795. It is entitled 'Copenhagen House', a popular venue for political gatherings in Islington. Quoting from Shakespeare, the speaker, who represents the London Corresponding Society, is proclaiming "I tell you, citizens, we mean to new-dress the Constitution and turn it, and set a new nap on it."
(Reproduced by kind permission of the Guildhall Library, Prints and Drawings, London)

On the back jacket is a Conservative Party poster of the 1920s, and a photograph of Ben Tillett addressing a meeting at Covent Garden.

Political
LONDON
a capital history

Richard Tames

HISTORICAL PUBLICATIONS

Contents

Introduction

Unlike many other national capitals London has never been a *purely* political city. Making money, rather than just extracting it from taxpayers, has always been central to its *raison d'etre*. This is a result of the divided locations of power in the capital, one being the ancient City, epicentre of commerce and finance, and the other, upstream on the Thames, Westminster, focal point of politics and parliamentary power. London for most of its history, has not been governed as a whole. Nor has it always been the national capital.

London *is* a political city and Londoners have at times intervened decisively to change the politics of the nation and even on occasion of the world – denying the throne to a pretender, rioting against an unpopular law, raising the cash for a war or defying the threats of an invader.

But London lacks the single-mindedness that is characteristic of purpose-built capitals. Washington was built on a swamp in a specially demarcated 'District of Columbia', to denote its separateness from the various states which constituted a newly independent America. Canberra was created to nullify the rivalry between Melbourne and Sydney. The point about Ottawa is that it isn't Toronto. Ankara, set on a plateau, bleak or baking according to the season, was chosen as the capital of the infant Turkish republic as a repudiation of the cosmopolitan heritage of Ottoman Istanbul. Brasilia was intended to tug Brazilians away from seductive coastal Rio and its historic orientation outward to Europe and Africa. Madrid and Tokyo similarly became capitals as a result of deliberate political choices which can be given a specific date.

London claims no specific date of foundation or historic founding figure. King Lud, unlike King Arthur or Robin Hood, has failed to impose himself on the popular imagination as a mythic founder so London has not even a fiction like Romulus to represent its origin, its spirit or its destiny. The city came into existence as a by-product of Roman military logistics and might have been snuffed out in infancy had the invaders not persevered in rebuilding it as their administrative base after it had been laid waste by the revolt of Queen Boudicca. As it was, *Londinium* remained a branch office of Rome rather than a city with an organic connection to its setting. When Rome could no longer garrison *Londinium*, it ceased to function. Its effective rebirth was the result of another deliberate political act, the decision of Alfred of Wessex to order its reoccupation and refortification in 886. London's continuous existence as a city dates from then and Alfred, if anyone, may be hailed as its post-Roman founder. But Alfred kept his capital at Winchester and it would be more than three centuries before a piecemeal process made Westminster the seat of monarchy and its adjuncts, the courts of justice, the bureaucracy and the periodic meetings of parliaments.

Since that time London has served as the central arena of the political life of the nation, a nation whose boundaries, definition, power and status have changed significantly over the centuries. The political life of London has, therefore, been simultaneously local, national and global, an overlapping of concerns reflected in the very names of hundreds of its streets and squares and the dedications of the monuments and memorials – and public houses – which recall its past.

This conjunction of the local and the global is neatly illustrated by two adjacent statues at the eastern end of Tooley Street in Bermondsey, where it runs into the approach road to Tower Bridge. One is of a cheery, corpulent Edward VII sort of figure, sporting a magnificent beard and moustache, arrayed in flowing robes and bearing a mayoral chain of office. Unless you happen to be from that area and to have a keen interest in its local history you – along with virtually every other Londoner – might be readily forgiven for failing to recognize Colonel Bevington, the first mayor of Bermondsey when it became established as a metropolitan borough in 1899 and a colonel by virtue of commanding the local company of Volunteer riflemen. Bermondsey's civic pride failed to set a trend and Bevington is the only purely local London politician to have been honoured with a statue, although Henry Reader Williams, a Hornsey politician, did merit a whole clock tower in Crouch End which perpetuates his memory. Just behind Col. Bevington is Ernest Bevin – creator of the Transport and General Workers' Union, wartime Minister of Labour, Foreign Secretary and architect of NATO – but he rates only a bust, marooned in a sad little mini-park, behind a grim block of public lavatories. The capital's political iconography entirely lacks the coherent rationale that underpins the self-representation of more ideologically-driven regimes.

What seems to matter about the politics of the past shifts with our own changing place in relation to both that past and our imagined future. It demands an effort of imaginative engagement by the modern secular mind to grasp how deeply for generations of Londoners religion and politics were inextricably interlinked, two sides of the same coin of monarchy. Short-term shifts in perspective can be equally significant. Writing in 1994 the late Roy Porter struck a note of almost apocalyptic gloom in the Introduction to his *London: A Social History*. The secure world of working-class New Cross which he knew as a child in the immediate post-war years he recognised as irretrievably lost along with smog and prefabs – and steady jobs down the docks. Deindustrialised, post-Thatcher London might be less grubby and more 'vibrant' but Porter regretted that it was no longer a place where the kids could play safely in the streets. Perhaps if he were writing now he might concede that, despite the fiasco of the Dome, the Millennium did do much to lift London's spirits and the prospect of hosting the 2012 Olympics has given it a new focus for the future.

The following pages offer a broadly chronological panorama of political events and illustrate how, in a city the size of London, there is invariably a quorum of discontent about something. A comprehensive and detailed account of London politics at the local, national *and* global levels is obviously beyond the scope of a single volume. Such aspects of political life as diplomacy, espionage and the role of the mass media, each worthy of treatment at book length, have of necessity been mentioned only in passing. The focus has been placed on the politics of the unavoidable – the happenings, personalities and institutions which even the most apolitical of Londoners could not fail to notice or to be affected by. The routines and processes of politics therefore take second place to their impact and outcomes and their representation as ritual, ceremony and display.

CHAPTER ONE

Capital Accumulation

Londinium

London has not always been the capital and only became so by stages. The Roman occupation of Britain which began in 43 AD initially made its notional capital at Colchester, where the emperor Claudius, nominal commander of the expedition, had received a symbolic act of submission from tribal leaders. A major temple, honouring Claudius as a god, was raised there. The rapid development of what became *Londinium*, around the major bridging-point on the Thames, soon, however, relegated Colchester to subsidiary status as a ritual centre for the celebration of the imperial cult.

Both Colchester and *Londinium* were devastated by Boudicca's revolt in AD 60-61.

Their immediate reconstruction was a fundamental political imperative, indicating both Roman determination to maintain a grip on the newly-acquired province of Britannia and the intrinsically civic nature of their rule. The task was entrusted to a newly-appointed procurator or fiscal supervisor, Classicianus, whose pragmatic policy was to promote prosperity rather than to impose punishment. A Gaul from Trier in what is now Germany, complete with a fictionalised genealogy claiming ancient Roman descent, Classicianus died in office *ca.* AD 65 and was buried beneath an imposing monument whose shattered remains were recovered piecemeal and by chance between the 1850s and the 1930s. The original is now in the British Museum and there are copies both at

1. A replica (left rear) of Classicianus' funeral monument set near a surviving section of Roman wall at Tower Hill. (The statue is an 18th-century bronze of Emperor Trajan, who never even visited Londinium – a somewhat misleading tribute to Roman rule.)

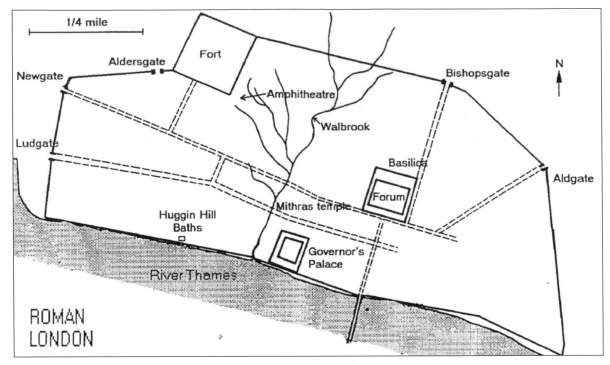

Map labels: 1/4 mile · Fort · Aldersgate · Newgate · N · Amphitheatre · Bishopsgate · Walbrook · Ludgate · Basilica · Aldgate · Forum · Mithras temple · Huggin Hill Baths · Governor's Palace · River Thames · ROMAN LONDON

2. A plan of the main features of Roman London so far discovered. The Forum and basilica are on the site of today's Leadenhall Market, and the fort is now occupied by the Museum of London and adjoining buildings. The amphitheatre, on the site of Guildhall Yard, was discovered in 1988 during the construction of the Guildhall Art Gallery.

Tower Hill and in the Museum of London.

Any knowledge of the political life of Roman *Londinium* must, in the absence of contemporary documentation, be largely a matter of inference and comparison with what is known of other Roman cities. The few mentions of the city that occur in Roman authors such as Tacitus and Dio Cassius add up to less than four pages of modern text. Epigraphic evidence is similarly scanty, amounting to only about three dozen inscriptions.

Londinium did become the largest and wealthiest provincial city of the western Roman empire north of the Alps, with a population that may at its peak have reached 100,000. Partly this reflects the city's significance as a commercial port. But its status and functions as a political centre are equally undoubted. Along the riverside, where Cannon Street station now stands, there was a building complex of palatial dimensions, dubbed 'Government House' by Dr. John Morris. This was almost certainly the residence and administrative headquarters of the provincial governor. Although the post of governor of Britannia was only a step on the ladder of a top-flight career, it was a much-prized one, attracting a succession of able men. Britannia was no backwater but a valued imperial possession. The limited terms served by senior Roman office-holders restricted the potential for corruption and the abuse of power which can accompany permanent tenure. Top men were essentially transients, accountable to Rome for their conduct of office, and they knew it. Government House supervised and sustained the basic infrastructure of imperial control – the collection of revenue, maintenance of roads and courier systems and the supply, payment and movement of troops. Subsidiary functions included the provision of hospitality to visiting dignitaries and local bigwigs and the maintenance of archives and a law library to help settle administrative queries and disputes. Roman government was aristocratic, political power being essentially a prerogative of the propertied. It was also authoritarian; but it was not arbitrary. Rules and records were fundamental to its method.

Opposite Government House stood the headquarters of the Provincial Council, through which local interests and sentiments could be consulted. 'City Hall' stood where Leadenhall Street and Bishopsgate now intersect. Its 500 foot long basilica, the largest building north of the Alps, combined the functions of town hall and law courts and was fronted by a forum, four times the size of Trafalgar Square, which served as a place of public assembly and market-place-cum-shopping-mall. Divided into wards, Roman London was run by councillors and magistrates drawn from the ranks of a propertied oligarchy by a mixture of election and co-optation. Their prime concern was the maintenance of good order i.e. the avoidance of palpable misgovernment, incompetence or corruption as these might be interpreted by the periodic inspection and auditing procedures co-ordinated ultimately from Rome itself.

Major civic responsibilities included the supervision of markets and the assurance of a supply of basic necessities, the provision of water-supply, public baths and street-cleansing, the maintenance of police and fire services, the licensing of craftsmen and traders and the upkeep of public buildings. Office-holding was both a prerogative of the propertied and a burden. Not only was it time-consuming and essentially unpaid, it also carried with it the expectation that office-holders would use their own personal fortunes to embellish the city and extend its civic facilities or at least to sponsor games in the amphitheatre, where regular, lavishly-staged recreations publicly affirmed the supremacy of the Roman gods and the respect due to the earthly representatives of their power.

Temples similarly functioned as settings for the attestation of loyalty to the imperial system. Christians were persecuted less for what they did believe than for what they didn't – in the divinity of the emperor. In the British Museum can be seen larger than life-size heads of the emperors Claudius, initial conqueror of Britannia and Hadrian, who made a tour of inspection in AD 122; these portrait busts are almost certainly the remnants of large public statues.

The area between Government House and City Hall accommodated many high-status buildings with mosaic floors, suggesting a residential district inhabited by the political class, its humbler buildings perhaps being the homes of locally-recruited clerical drones. Buildings of intermediate status may have housed members of skilled service industries such as doctors and tutors. Although Roman *Londinium* boasted few parks it was also disfigured by few of the squalid high-rise tenement blocks which were so marked a feature of Rome itself.

Londinium's fort stood at the north-east corner of the city, roughly where the Museum of London is now, the base of one its towers still being visible towards the southern end of Noble Street. Given the Romans' confidence that they had the south and east of Britain firmly under control it was less a citadel than a barracks and depot. Legionaries arriving for a tour of duty from warmer climes might well have passed through it to get kitted out with suitable clothing. More permanent occupants would have supplied the governor with his guard and performed policing duties on the streets and at the gates of the city.

At the end of the second century the smooth running of Roman *Londinium* was disrupted by the outbreak of civil war which reverberated throughout the provinces of the empire. As a frontier outpost Britain always had at least three legions permanently stationed, plus locally-recruited auxiliaries, amounting perhaps to a tenth or more of the Roman army. Despite being on the edge of a world focused on the Mediterranean, Britain was therefore a promising base from which to launch a bid for power. In AD 193 governor Clodius Albinus did just that, taking most of his forces to fight on the Continent. Roman London's walls date from this period of crisis, possibly begun on the orders of the rebellious governor to secure his rear base. In any case they were completed at the behest of his conqueror, the legitimate emperor, Septimius Severus, who secured Britannia in person and died at York in 211. Britain became divided into two provinces, with *Londinium*, capital of Britannia Superior as a primarily administrative centre and York (*Eboracum*), capital of Britannia Inferior, functioning mainly as a focal point for military operations.

Disorder returned in 286 when Carausius, commander of the Channel fleet, declared himself emperor and established a London mint to turn Saxon pirate booty into coinage to buy the loyalty of local troops. In 293 Carausius was murdered by his finance officer, Allectus, who was in turn overthrown by the rightful ruler, Constantius Chlorus. His timely arrival in the capital, ahead of the remnants of Allectus' defeated forces, was hailed by its inhabitants as a deliverance from an almost certain sack. The first known representation of London to survive is a gold medallion, found at Arras in France, showing the strongly-gated city welcoming the 'Restorer of Eternal Light'. In reality the city actually depicted was probably Trier, where the piece was struck. Whatever its lack of authenticity in strictly topographical terms the fact remains that the first depiction of London was occasioned by a political crisis and produced as a political affirmation.

Although fourth-century *Londinium* was past its demographic and commercial peak the despatch of high-ranking generalissimos like Theodosius and Stilicho to supervise the refortification of the city shows that Rome clearly intended to hold onto it. As if to boost morale in the face of a deteriorating security situation the city was also granted the honorific title 'Augusta'. The end, when it came, was entirely precipitated by political factors. Stilicho's execution as a result of palace politics in 408 led to a security crisis in Italy itself, precipitating the withdrawal of the legions and, consequently, the cessation of their pay – which had always been the major driver of the monetized sector of the provincial economy. How long a quasi-Roman administration was maintained in Londinium is not known. Writing around 500 AD Zosimus recorded that the British had "revolted from Roman rule and lived by themselves; no longer obeying Roman laws".

Lundenwic and Lundenburg

With the departure of the legions history with a capital H also left London. The disintegration of a unified, if only superficially Romanized, Britannia was accompanied by the evaporation of centralised political control. When urban life resumed in London the city would become a prize for the contending kingdoms which eventually emerged from the settlement of the country by Anglo-Saxon newcomers, variously under the sway of Essex, Kent, Mercia or, in the end, Wessex. In Rome itself London appears to have maintained its reputation as a place that mattered because, when Pope Gregory the Great despatched St. Augustine to reintroduce Christianity to the former Roman possession in 597 his instructions included the command to establish a see in London. This was duly done by 604, the traditional date for the foundation of St. Paul's cathedral. The pagan Londoners, however, proved hostile, driving out bishop Mellitus. The king of Kent, by contrast, proved welcoming and so Canterbury, by default, became the primary spiritual centre of the future England.

London as a settlement was reconstituted outside the Roman walls, upstream to the west, on the bend of the river Thames around what is now Charing Cross. This was *Lundenwic*, a place of trade rather than a citadel. Its political life may reasonably be conjectured as a minimal framework required by a commercial community for maintaining order, enforcing contracts and resolving disputes. A charter of Frithuwold of Surrey of *ca.* 672-4 refers to "the port of London, where ships come to land". Writing *ca.* 730 AD the monastic chronicler Bede of remote Jarrow, still knew it by reputation as "the mart of many nations". Mercia levied tolls at London during the following decade and later in the century coins were issued there. Offa the Great of Mercia may have occupied a royal palace in what is now the area of Wood Street as an occasional residence and there may have been some sort of administrative presence in what was left of the Roman fort at Cripplegate. Further upstream from Lundenwic a monastery came into existence. A charter issued by Offa in 785 confirmed the river Tyburn as marking one of the boundaries of this 'West Minster'.

The unification of England into a single kingdom was achieved by the royal house of Wessex, whose capital was at Winchester. London was raided by Vikings in 841, presumably because it was wealthy enough to make the risks and costs worthwhile. The Vikings returned in 851 and occupied it over the winter of 871-872. In 886 Alfred the Great of Wessex (reigned 871-99) ordered the reoccupation and refortification of London, primarily for it to serve as the easternmost anchor-point for the diagonal defensive line of garrisoned strong-points – *burhs* – which he had established to protect territories still under English control from further Viking encroachment. *Lundenwic*, the marketplace, had been superseded by *Lundenburg*, the fortress. The importance that Alfred attached to London was signified by his decision to place it under the command of his own son-in-law, Ethelred, as 'Ealdorman'. London would henceforth play a pivotal role in the processes of state-formation and nation-building.

How Anglo-Saxon London was governed remains largely a matter of speculation. But the division of the city into its present wards quite possibly emerges in this period, as may the office of alderman, which probably originated as the captain of a militia unit organised on a ward-by-ward basis. The office of sheriff, originally reeve, the representative of royal authority in the city, is also of pre-Conquest origin. The Viking contribution was a consultative assembly which met indoors – the husting ('house thing'). A larger assembly, the folkmoot, seems to have been convened less often and outdoors and had the sole authority to proclaim malefactors as outlaws. Criminality was curbed by the institution of the frith guild, a sort of authorised system of vigilantism. Important religious institutions and some leading families exercised their own jurisdiction over autonomous residential enclaves in their possession, known as sokes.

By 1016 the *Anglo-Saxon Chronicle* established by Alfred could record that Edmund Ironside was chosen king by "all the lords who were in London and the citizens". Edmund failed even to see out that year but his Danish successor confirmed London as the political base from which to rule a maritime empire that stretched across the North Sea to Scandinavia, a practice continued by Knut's sons and successors, Harald and Harthacnut. When the succession reverted to the Anglo-Saxon royal house in the person of Edward the Confessor he chose to devote his energies to rebuilding Westminster Abbey, establishing a new royal palace nearby from which to supervise the project. This upstream Versailles in miniature would become the epicentre of royal rule, existing in tension with the ancient fortified city downstream, the powerhouse of the metropolitan economy and an essential source of governmental income from taxes, tolls and loans.

The Confessor's chosen celibacy guaranteed a succession crisis at his death, bloodily resolved by the defeat of his brother-in-law Harold Godwineson at the hands of his cousin, Duke William of Normandy. Despite his decisive triumph at the battle for Senlac ridge near Hastings William the Conqueror (reigned 1066-87) was sufficiently wary of London not to attack it but to wait for its submission and to give a written guarantee of the continuity of its institutions – "I will that you be worthy of all the laws you were worthy of in the time of King Edward. And I will that every child shall be his father's heir after his father's day. And I will not suffer any man to do you wrong. God preserve you." A change of management was, however, unambiguously signified by the construction of a massive new royal stronghold across the eastern boundary wall of the city – the Tower of London.

Crown and Corporation

Over the course of succeeding centuries the City strove to achieve increased autonomy from royal interference, sometimes utilising its military strength but more often its financial leverage, to wring concessions from the occupant of the throne – and sometimes to determine who that occupant should be.

Some time towards the end of his long reign Henry I (reigned 1100-1135) granted the City a

Tower of Power

London guides are taught to memorize the different purposes which have been served by the Tower of London by using the mnemonic MOZART. It has housed the Royal MINT and Royal OBSERVATORY, Royal ZOO and Royal ARCHIVES and served as a Royal RESIDENCE and still serves as a Royal TREASURE HOUSE. But the most famous function of the Tower has been to serve as a political prison.

William I began the construction of the Tower of London for political as well as strategic purposes, not only to defend the passage to London Bridge but to overawe the inhabitants of the largest city of his newly-conquered country. Standing over 90 feet high and built deliberately athwart the City's walls, what was to become known as the White Tower was a proclamation of dominance, statement architecture of the most unambiguous kind. Although much of the material used was local Kentish rag, the constructional strength depended on stone brought from Caen in William's native Normandy, underlining the alien nature of this unfamiliar addition to London's skyline. Henry I added a free-standing chapel, appropriately dedicated to St. Peter Ad Vincula – St. Peter in Chains. Rebuilt by Henry VIII in 1520, the chapel was to become the last resting-place of his second wife, Anne Boleyn, and of dozens of other victims of monarchical malevolence. Henry II added a kitchen, bakery and gaol. During Richard I's reign a curtain wall was begun and the Bell Tower was built. The elaboration and completion of the main structure was largely the work of Henry III and Edward I. Henry III added an imposing Great Hall (long gone) and the moat, filled in as a health hazard in 1843 on the orders of the then Constable, the Duke of Wellington. A spendthrift aesthete, Henry III also ordered the central keep to be whitewashed, hence its name, the White Tower, even though it no longer is. Edward I built the Beauchamp, Byward and Lion Towers and Traitors' Gate. Henry VIII constructed the attractive half-timbered range which now accommodates the Resident Governor. He also added two artillery bastions which, significantly, face inward, towards the City. Wren built the Grand Storehouse and remodelled the windows of the White Tower, After the terrible fire of 1841, which gutted the Grand Armoury, the Wellington Barracks block was built in its place; it now houses the Crown Jewels, the ultimate in royal bling.

The Tower of London was first used as a regular royal residence by Stephen but it was the self-indulgent Henry III who gave it the splendour and comfort befitting a king. It was also during his reign that the royal menagerie was established. Exotic animals were an adjunct of diplomacy, a demonstration of the generosity of the giver. The king of Norway sent a polar bear. The king of France trumped him with an elephant. James I, the last monarch to use the Tower as a regular royal residence, took a malicious pleasure in staging fights between lions and bears or tormenting them with mastiffs. The royal menagerie was despatched to join the newly-established Zoological Gardens in Regent's Park in 1835.

The Tower was first used as a prison in 1101 when Ranulf Flambard, bishop of Durham, was arrested for corruption. Having got his guards drunk, he escaped from a window by a rope. The portly Welsh prince Llewellyn was less fortunate in attempting the same method, falling to his death. In 1278 Edward I, recently returned from Crusade and apparently fired with religious bigotry, had 600 Jews imprisoned for alleged coin-clipping. The following year 267 of them were hanged and the rest banished. In 1303 the abbot of Westminster and eighty other suspects were imprisoned after the theft of items of royal regalia from Westminster Abbey; ever since then the Crown Jewels have been kept at the Tower. During the Hundred Years War against France distinguished prisoners included David II, king of Scotland and John II, king of France, who was held for three years while his enormous ransom was raised. In 1399, having deposed his cousin Richard II, Henry Bolingbroke spent the eve of his coronation in the Tower, spiritually cleansed by a ceremonial bath, thus inaugurating the Order of the Bath.

During the Wars of the Roses the deranged Henry VI was held in the Tower for six years,

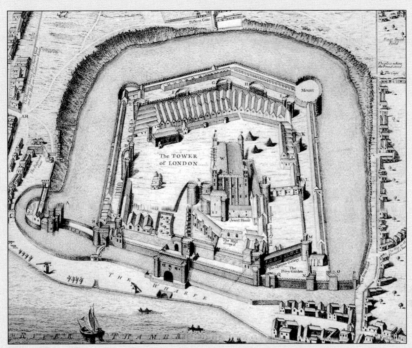

3. *The Tower by the end of the 16th century. The scaffold is top left and the Lion Tower, which housed the royal menagerie, is bottom left. The Jewel House, south of the White Tower has now gone. Most of the moat was a dry ditch.*

rescued, restored to his throne, recaptured and died, probably murdered, while at the *prie-dieu* in the Wakefield Tower. The equally hapless child-king Edward V and his brother the Duke of York – 'the little princes in the Tower' – were almost certainly murdered in the Garden (now Bloody) Tower in 1483, probably on the orders of their uncle, who became Richard III. The bodies of two boys were uncovered near the White Tower in the reign of Charles II and re-interred in Westminster Abbey on his orders.

From Edward I's reign onwards the coronation procession departed from the Tower to wend its way to Westminster Abbey. Edward threw coins to the crowds as the conduits ran with wine. In 1377 ten-year-old Richard II rode forth dressed in white robes like a miniature angel. When Henry V's procession set off in an April snowstorm royal spin-doctors optimistically interpreted the unseasonal phenomenon as confirmation that the king "had put off the winter of his youth". Henry VII was the first to be attended by the newly-formed Yeomen of the Guard.

Henry VIII marked his joint coronation with Catherine of Aragon by creating 24 new Knights of the Bath. The last sovereign to ride in procession to his coronation from the Tower was Charles II.

The bloodiest phase of the Tower's history was under the Tudors, when the unity of the kingdom was threatened by internal uprisings, faction, intrigue and disturbing religious ideas, as well as the more traditional problems of dynastic ambitions and hostility from neighbouring states. Henry VII was not inclined to vindictiveness but doubtless regarded the extinction of the last Plantagenet claimant as mere prudence. Henry VIII inaugurated his reign by executing his father's hated tax-gatherers, Empson and Dudley. Subsequent victims included the principled Sir Thomas More, the frail Bishop Fisher, the enforcer of his reformation, Thomas Cromwell and the king's second and fifth wives, Anne Boleyn and Catherine Howard. Under Elizabeth there was a steady procession of Jesuit priests and at the end of the reign the queen had to order the execution of her own favourite, the youthful Earl of Essex after his

4. The church of St Peter ad Vincula in the 1890s. The site of the scaffold is to the left foreground. Most executions – over 120 – took place on Tower Hill, outside the Tower's perimeter.

abortive attempt at a putsch. Essex's courtly rival Sir Walter Raleigh, looked on, doubtless with ill-concealed relish, but ended up as a prisoner in the Tower himself for over a decade after being implicated in an alleged plot against James I.

In 1685, following the defeat of his attempted seizure of the throne, Charles II's eldest bastard son, James, Duke of Monmouth, was consigned to the Tower before his botched execution on Tower Hill. In 1716 the Jacobite Lord Nithsdale, despite being six feet tall, escaped from the Tower on the eve of his execution, disguised as his wife's maid. The Jacobite aristocrats imprisoned after the failure of the '45 were less fortunate. Lord Cromarty was pardoned because he was only nineteen. Lord Tullibardine died in captivity, but Lords Kilmarnock and Balmerino perished on Tower Hill, as did Lord Lovat, the last person to be executed there by the axe. The last executions at Tower Hill, in 1780, by hanging, were those of a one-armed ex-soldier and a prostitute, in retribution for their alleged roles in the Gordon Riots.

The Tower of London was revived as a place of confinement for political prisoners in the twentieth century. Sir Roger Casement, found guilty of treason for his role in planning the 1916 Easter Rising in Dublin, was imprisoned in St. Thomas's Tower before being hanged at Pentonville. A total of eleven spies were shot in the outer ward by the Martin Tower. During World War Two Hitler's deputy, Rudolf Hess, was held in the Lieutenant's House for four days. The last person to be executed in the Tower was a German spy, shot in the rifle-range which then existed in the moat, in 1941.

The Tower's current incarnation as a visitor attraction dates from at least the sixteenth century and was primarily political in origin and purpose. Privileged visitors were shown the contents of what was known as the 'Spanish Armoury' and told that the weapons on display had all been seized by the English from their defeated enemies. To this was added a propagandist and wildly unhistorical 'Line of Kings' in which William the Conqueror appeared complete with a firearm. But although the Tower is now only ever besieged by souvenir-seeking tourists, it remains, as Pevsner reminds us "the most important work of military architecture in England."

royal charter confirming its right to elect its own Sheriffs (usually two), who were responsible for tax collection, rather than a royal appointee imposed on it. Citizens were also exempted from the obligation to provide hospitality to the royal household. If Henry's motive was to gain pre-emptive support for the succession of his daughter, Matilda, the ploy failed. When Henry died the City chose to throw its support behind the usurper Stephen of Blois. In 1141 Stephen forsook the security of the Tower and was taken by his enemies at Lincoln. A synod convened at Winchester by its bishop – Stephen's own turncoat brother – claimed the right to confirm Matilda as sovereign. Matilda's highhandedness on coming to London for her intended coronation provoked the Londoners into an uprising which drove her out and denied her the sacral ceremony. Stephen rewarded this intervention by recognising London as a self-governing commune. When, at Stephen's death, the throne, by agreement, passed to Matilda's son as Henry II he deemed it prudent to issue a charter confirming that London's citizens could not be tried beyond its walls and were free of all tolls outside them. The establishment of the office of mayor likewise dates, significantly, from the beginning of the reign of Richard I (reigned 1189-99), a largely absentee monarch anxious to secure the richest city of his realms before departing on crusade. At the end of his reign the Lionheart's brother and successor, John (reigned 1199-1216), trying to face down a major baronial revolt, granted London a new charter which introduced the principle of an annually elected mayor. Over the succeeding century the holders of this office would achieve seniority over the sheriffs, serving not only as the City's chief magistrate, administrator and legislator but also as the personification of its corporate identity.

The Conqueror's successors maintained such a nomadic style of government that the capital was, in effect, wherever the king happened to be. By the early thirteenth century, however, the volume of governmental business was such that Westminster became established as a permanent bureaucratic base *(see p. 22)*. As if in affirmation

of this the Archbishop of Canterbury also chose to establish a permanent residence nearby – Lambeth Palace.

Although the principle of an annually elected mayor had been established there was no bar to an individual serving more than one term. Between 1214 and 1337 fourteen mayors held office on multiple occasions, ranging from three to no less than eight times. The celebrated Dick Whittington (died 1423) was the last medieval mayor to serve more than two terms of office. Mayors were drawn from the City's ruling elite of aldermen. Guyed in later centuries as pompous figures of fun, London's medieval aldermen, serving for life, wielded such awesome authority that the penalty for striking one was the loss of the offending hand. Aldermen stood at the apex of the City's commercial hierarchy. Many were engaged in the import or export of commodities. Often they had profitable connections with the royal court as suppliers of luxuries such as furs, fine textiles, gems, armour, wines or spices. Command of numeracy enabled many to hold office as royal servants in the Exchequer or the Wardrobe. The bulk of the active citizenry were property-holding members of the city's craft and merchant guilds, known as livery companies from the dress they wore on ceremonial occasions. Consulted en masse on occasion, they were also liable to serve in rotation at parochial level in such offices as constable or watchman.

The closing years of the long reign of Henry III (reigned 1216-72) were marked by open conflict between the monarch and the City. The king's lavish expenditure on the rebuilding of Westminster Abbey and the elaboration of the Tower of London necessitated heavy taxation. His favouritism towards the alien entourage of his Provencal queen aroused xenophobic resentment. Henry's decision in 1245 to authorise two annual fairs at Westminster added a further economic grievance. In 1263 Londoners actually dared to pelt Queen Eleanor with rubbish as she passed under London Bridge en route to the Tower. During the subsequent baronial uprising against royal rule London chose to side with the rebel faction led by Simon

Lord Mayor

The City's Chief Magistrate, chairman of the Courts of Aldermen and Common Council and Admiral of the Port of London, was originally known simply as the Mayor. The office, first mentioned in 1189, was initially held by Henry Fitzailwyn until his death in 1212. He was the only Mayor to hold the office for life. The rapid acceptance of the importance of the Mayoralty is confirmed by the fact that of the twenty-five people who put their seal to the Magna Carta in 1215 the Mayor, Roger FitzAlan, was the only commoner. In that same year King John confirmed by charter the right of London's citizens to elect their own mayor. The term Lord Mayor is first recorded in 1283 and became habitual from *ca.* 1545.

For centuries the City's Mayoralty was dominated by the Twelve Great Livery Companies with office-holding rotating between Mercers, Grocers, Drapers, Fishmongers, Goldsmiths etc. Oligarchic in structure, the City's mercantile elite was nevertheless remarkably permeable to talent, notably extra-metropolitan talent. Of the hundred occupants of the office of Lord Mayor during the sixteenth century nine-tenths had been born outside the City. Many, moreover, either retained strong links with their places of origin, posthumously expressed in terms of bequests such as the foundation of almshouses and schools or were eager to acquire country properties and embellish them. These tendencies inhibited the formation of the sort of self-perpetuating and exclusive mercantile elite more characteristic of, say, Bristol.

In times of political confrontation the Lord Mayor has often been expected to defend the liberties of the City and sometimes to speak for the nation. Access to the levers of financial power has also enabled a Lord Mayor to influence royal policy and even changes of dynasty, as in the case of Sir Anthony Clayton who denied support to James II while mobilising it for William III. Other significant examples of Mayoral interventions include those of William Beckford, Brass Crosby and Robert Waithman.

William Beckford (1709-70) is the only Lord Mayor honoured with a statue in Guildhall. Heir to the greatest sugar fortune in Jamaica, a brilliant pupil at Westminster and Oxford, a medical student at Leyden and Paris, Beckford would become the owner of thirteen plantations and three thousand slaves. After a decade in colonial estate management and politics, Beckford settled in London to become the City's MP until his death and to serve twice as Lord Mayor. In an age of conspicuous self-indulgence Beckford's mayoralty was remarkable for the sumptuousness of its entertainments. Beckford's personal abstemiousness was, by contrast, noteworthy but purely dietary – he fathered six sons and two daughters out of wedlock. An intimate of the elder Pitt, Beckford vigorously defended planter interests in Parliament but also supported his mentor's opposition to governmental abuses of power.

In March 1770 Beckford, as Mayor, accompanied by a full panoply of attendant Aldermen and Common Councilmen, marched from Guildhall to St. James's Palace to petition George III against his support for the government's action in interfering in the Middlesex by-election which had elected John Wilkes *(see p. 65),* declaring instead for his opponent. On a second occasion, in May, Beckford repeated the remonstrance and did not hesitate to lecture the astonished monarch on his alleged constitutional impropriety. Beckford died just four weeks later and his supporters voted him a statue in his honour. It depicts him in his robes of office, delivering his speech to the king, the text of which is inscribed on the plinth in letters of gold. The effete but acute Horace Walpole dismissed Beckford as the epitome of the *nouveaux riches* – vulgar and vainglorious, at best a "noisy good humoured flatterer". Pitt, by contrast, congratulated Beckford's unprecedented reproof to his sovereign as having "asserted the City with weight and Spirit", declaring that "the spirit of old England spoke, that never to be forgotten day."

Born on Teesside and trained as a lawyer, Brass Crosby (1725-93) accumulated a personal fortune by three successive marriages to rich widows and bought and swiftly sold the office of City Remembrancer, before becoming an MP

5. *William Beckford.*

7. *The Waithman obelisk in Salisbury Square.*

6. *The procession by river of the Lord Mayor to Westminster in 1789. Oil painting by Richard Paton and Francis Wheatley.*

8. *The Lord Mayor had his ceremonial coach – this is now displayed in the Museum of London. But for day-to-day use, before the time of motor cars, he had another distinguished vehicle. It is seen here outside a house called Fairseat in Highgate Village c.1872, the home of the Lord Mayor, Sir Sydney Waterlow.*

9. *Today's mayoral car.*

and in 1770 Lord Mayor. An enthusiastic partisan of John Wilkes, on taking office Crosby ostentatiously declared that he would stake his life on protecting the liberties and privileges of the City. One of his first acts was to refuse to enforce Admiralty warrants for the press-gang. He then refused to convict City printers of violating parliamentary privilege by reporting debates. Summoned to the Commons and confined to the Tower for his defiance, Crosby became a national hero, feted by a stream of visitors. Released when the parliamentary session closed, Crosby returned to the Mansion House in a triumphal procession, having at least indirectly secured the right to report parliamentary debates, Although he failed twice more to regain his seat in Parliament, Crosby became Governor of the Irish Society and at the time of his death was also chairman of four City committees. An obelisk erected in his honour now stands outside the Imperial War Museum in Lambeth.

Welsh by birth, Robert Waithman (1764-1833) became a wealthy draper and liveryman of the Framework Knitters' Company. Politicised by the French revolution, he opposed war against France and founded the Society of the Independent Livery of London to lobby against it and for the repeal of income tax and the reform of parliament. While continuing to attack official incompetence and campaigning for reform and a free press, Crosby was careful to distance himself from radicals espousing violence. Briefly MP for the City, Waithman served as sheriff in 1820-1 and Lord Mayor in 1823-4. Re-elected in 1826, he retained his seat in the elections of 1830, 1831 and 1832 but died poor. After Waithman's burial in St. Bride's, an obelisk was erected in his honour at the southern end of Farringdon Street. It was relocated to Bartholomew Close in 1951 and to Salisbury Square in 1972.

The Lord Mayor is elected annually on Michaelmas Day (September 29th) and must have served as Sheriff. He is admitted to office on the Friday before the second Saturday in November in a ceremony known as 'the Silent Change' in which the paraphernalia of office – sword, mace, purse etc. – are passed to the new incumbent in complete silence. The Lord Mayor's Show takes place the following day. Apart from presiding over the administration of the City the Lord Mayor's major function in the twenty-first century is to promote it as the world's leading international financial centre and to further the interests of the UK's financial services sector as a whole. His other offices include serving as Chancellor of City University and President of the City of London Territorial and Volunteer Reserve.

The Lord Mayor's Banquet has been held in Guildhall in honour of the outgoing Lord Mayor for at least four centuries and now takes place on the Monday after the Lord Mayor's Show. The guests invariably include the Prime Minister who delivers a speech reviewing Britain's international position.

The Lord Mayor's coach, built in 1757 to the designs of Sir Robert Taylor for £1,065, is decorated with panel paintings by Giovanni Battista Cipriani. These represent Faith, Hope and Charity (front), the Genius of the City with Riches, Plenty, Neptune, Trade and Commerce (back), the Genius with Fame (right) and with Mars (left). Weighing 2 tons 17 cwts, the coach had no brakes until 1951. Housed in the Museum of London, the coach is brought out annually for the Lord Mayor's Show.

King John's charter of 1215 required a new Mayor to be presented to the sovereign for approval and to swear fealty, a process necessitating a journey from the City to the seat of royal power in Westminster. By 1401 this had become an elaborate procession with aldermen and minstrels. From 1422 until 1856 the new Mayor went by water, and colourful pageants were staged for the occasion from the sixteenth century, often featuring exotic beasts, such as camels. Since at least 1566 the procession has been co-ordinated by an appointed Pageantmaster. The last procession to go right to Westminster Hall was in 1882; since then the presentation ceremony has taken place at the new Royal Courts of Justice in the Strand. To avoid traffic congestion in 1959 the procession was switched from October 29th to the second Saturday in November. The Show nowadays incorporates a theme chosen by the Lord Mayor and takes more than a year in the planning. In the Millennium Year the procession involved 6,500 participants, sixty floats, two hundred horses and twenty carriages.

de Montfort and took advantage of the king's capture at the battle of Lewes to attack 'the king's Jews', killing some five hundred. Following de Montfort's defeat and death at the battle of Evesham at the hands of the king's redoubtable son, 'the Lord Edward', retribution was imposed with a swingeing fine of 20,000 marks and the suspension of the City's liberties for a period of two years.

When Edward became king he made a point of further strengthening the Tower as evidence of his intent to reassert royal authority and crack down on corruption and disorder. In 1285 direct royal control of the city's administration was imposed with the appointment of paid officials and record-keeping set on a systematic basis. At the same time the patrician elite was opened up to new mercantile interests such as members of the Fishmongers' and Skinners' companies. Only in 1298 were the mayoralty and charter fully reinstated.

A new charter issued in 1319 under Edward's son and successor, Edward II (reigned 1307-27), confirmed that the mayor of London was to serve office for a single year and decreed that aldermen were also to be elected annually and not serve for two consecutive years. It also confirmed the right of craft guilds to control entry to their membership. London's decision to intervene decisively against the king in 1326 during the final baronial struggle which led to Edward II's overthrow gave a mob the chance to behead the unpopular royal treasurer, the bishop of Exeter, and to ransack the houses of Lombard merchants who, since the expulsion of the Jewish community in 1290, had replaced them as money-lenders. London was rewarded by the extension of the City's authority across the river to include the prosperous suburb of Southwark and by the imposition of restrictions on the activities of alien merchants.

During the long reign of Edward III (reigned 1327-77) London benefited from the king's war for the throne of France but was severely disrupted by the impact of the Black Death, which carried off at least a third of the city's population in 1349 and returned again in 1361

and periodically thereafter, creating an immense labour shortage. Bargaining strength swung decisively away from the privileged and the propertied while the burden of war became increasingly onerous. When Richard II (reigned 1377-99) came to the throne aged ten his advisers decided to balance the budget by imposing a poll tax, which largely exempted those who could afford to pay it and threw the consequent burden onto the mass of the population. The third such imposition, in 1381, was met with widespread evasion. Attempts to enforce compliance provoked outright rebellion. What became known as the Peasants' Revolt broke out in Essex and led to contingents from that county and from Kent converging on London.

Outbreaks of violence occurred at many other places but London became the major arena of confrontation. Londoners, initially sympathising with the rebels, opened the gates to admit them. The Tower garrison obligingly handed over the Archbishop of Canterbury, Simon of Sudbury, and the Treasurer, Sir Robert Hales, Prior of the Hospitallers, who were held to be the chief architects of the oppressive tax and were dragged to Tower Hill for summary execution. The mob then attacked Lambeth Palace and destroyed the Palace of the Savoy, home of the king's uncle, John of Gaunt, seen as a malign power behind the throne. The Hospitallers' priory at Clerkenwell was also sacked. The Marshalsea, Fleet and Newgate prisons were liberated of their inmates. Lawyers in the Inns of Court, widely hated as the instruments of feudal servitude, were arbitrarily murdered. Londoners also took advantage of the mayhem to massacre industrious Flemish immigrants. Practically the only person to keep a cool head was the boy king, who met rebel contingents on the fringes of the city, at Greenwich, at Mile End and finally at Smithfield. There the most prominent of the rebel ringleaders, Wat Tyler, provoked the royal entourage sufficiently to strike him a lethal blow. With astonishing self-possession and a skilfully ambiguous turn of phrase – "You shall have no other Captain but me" – the teenage monarch

10. The slaying of Wat Tyler by the Lord Mayor, William Walworth.

persuaded the mob to disperse peacefully. Once the rebels had returned to their villages and towns relentless royal retribution followed on their heels. But no further poll taxes were ever imposed.

Londoners, particularly propertied ones, were doubtless grateful to Richard II for reimposing order but their loyalty was not permanent. As the king became increasingly authoritarian and arbitrary he forfeited popular goodwill as well as fuelling baronial animosity. When the hated John of Gaunt died in 1399 Richard was away in Ireland attempting to subdue rebellion. Gaunt's son, Henry Bolingbroke, took advantage of the hiatus to return from exile in France and forward a somewhat implausible claim to the throne. The mayor headed a crowd of Londoners which escorted the usurper into the City, decreed the day a public holiday and put 1,200 men at Henry's disposal. Richard, having lost the support of his capital, submitted to his deposition. The City was to play an equally decisive role in bringing Edward IV to the throne during the Wars of the Roses in 1461.

London's prosperity in the fifteenth century was symbolized by the construction of its magnificent Guildhall between 1411 and 1440. The City's sense of civic identity was simultaneously enshrined in text by its long-serving Common Clerk, John Carpenter, whose *Liber Albus* (White Book) recorded in detail its customs and ordinances. The mayoralty and aldermanate continued to be dominated by members of the 'Twelve Great Companies'. Of eighty-eight persons who served as mayor no less than sixty-one were Mercers, Grocers or Drapers, companies which between them also supplied more than a third of all aldermen.

London's security was briefly threatened in 1450 when local abuses of power in Kent led to a march of the aggrieved on London. Led by one Jack Cade, of whom little more is known than his name, the Kentish men were reinforced by a contingent from Essex. Initially their ire was concentrated on unpopular royal servants but when they turned to looting the Londoners turned on them and beat them out of the City. Cade fled his temporary headquarters at the White Hart in Southwark, was tracked down, decapitated and dismembered and his remains trundled through the City on a hurdle as a reminder of the price of unsuccessful treason.

CHAPTER TWO

Monarchy, Modest and Magnificent

Under the Tudor dynasty monarchy as a system of personal government reached its apogee. Unlike their continental rivals the Tudors never tried to abolish their parliaments but managed them to achieve their purposes. Parliament – or rather parliaments – remained an occasion and a process rather than a permanent organ of state. Ruling through a combination of judicial violence and judicious patronage, Tudor monarchs used the powers of an increasingly effective machinery of state to shape the loyalties and lives of their subjects more closely than any of their medieval predecessors. Only a few buildings remain in London as physical testimony of their sway but they changed for ever the way their people understood themselves as a nation.

Henry VII (reigned 1485-1509)

Derided as a monarch so colourless that he never even got a nickname, Henry VII ended a quarter century of civil war to establish a quarter century of peace, negotiated trade treaties greatly beneficial to London, inaugurated its career as hub of empire by claiming England's first non-European territory, appropriately dubbed Newfoundland, and left his throne to an adult male with a treasury in healthy surplus. The king also saw off repeated plots and coups on behalf of pretenders with foreign backing and, as late as 1497 crushed an army of Cornish rebels at Blackheath.

Henry was the first English monarch whose portrait attempted a real likeness of the man and whose coins showed more than just a stylized representation of a king. The military unit established for his coronation, the Yeomen of the Guard, is claimed to be the oldest royal

12. Henry VII.

bodyguard and military corps in continuous existence in the world. A brave warrior, devout Christian and faithful husband, Henry established in perpetuity the principle of legitimacy in the succession to the throne, every subsequent English monarch being descended from his line.

Henry's claim to the throne by descent was real but indirect. Having literally seized the crown at the battle of Bosworth, he went straight to London where the Mayor and Aldermen escorted him to St. Paul's to hear a solemn *Te Deum*. Henry then buttressed his success by

13. Baynard's Castle at Blackfriars, rebuilt by Henry VII.

statutory confirmation in Parliament and by marrying – in gracious obedience to a joint petition of Lords and Commons – Elizabeth of York, daughter of Edward IV, to reconcile the defeated Yorkist faction.

Almost uniquely for a medieval monarch Henry VII liked paperwork. Detailed annotations to official documentation, particularly financial data, prove his diligence. He acquired a reputation for being mean but knew that magnificence was an essential attribute of successful kingship. He did, however, develop the knack of getting others – such as London's merchant oligarchs – to stump up much of the costs for such occasions as welcoming his future daughter-in-law, Catherine of Aragon or the funeral of his own consort.

Henry extended the royal residence at Greenwich, rebuilt Baynard's Castle as a *pied-a-terre* for central London and created a splendid new showpiece upriver at Sheen after the old palace was destroyed by fire in 1498. This he named Richmond after his Yorkshire earldom.

Henry's most lavish project, however, was the stunning chapel at the eastern end of Westminster Abbey, originally intended to house the remains and to perpetuate the memory of the murdered and saintly Henry VI, whose canonisation he also sought. In the event it was to become Henry VII's own resting-place and to be known by his name.

Henry VIII (reigned 1509-1547)

Henry VIII set out to dazzle his subjects and his rival monarchs and, in his youth and prime, he did. In Hans Holbein (?1497-1543) he found an artist of the first European rank to shape an iconic image of kingship which still adorns pub-signs from one end of England to the other. The image was, moreover, based on substance. Standing six feet four inches, the king literally towered over his subjects. A fearless jouster, a fine archer, a keen tennis player, Henry was also a gifted musician and a more than competent scholar. Unlike his father, however, Henry had little appetite for administration and was more

21. The burning of John Rogers, vicar of St. Sepulchre's, in 1555.

Edward's religious laws, but reversing the despoliation of the church had already become unthinkable. Reformist bishops, however, she could and did suspend. Statutes against heresy were revived and the authority of the Pope acknowledged.

Mary's determination to marry Philip II of Spain, master of the most powerful Catholic state in the world, was motivated by her desire to provide England with a successor to her throne committed to her personal crusade to restore the country to the Roman faith. Aged thirty-seven she had no time to lose. A Kentish gentleman Sir Thomas Wyatt (?1521-54) led a march of four thousand men on London to scotch the project by force but Mary held firm and the Lord Mayor refused to open Ludgate to the insurrection. Wyatt, taken at Temple Bar, was executed at Tower Hill. The Spanish marriage went ahead

and proved both barren and disastrous.

In 1555 the queen began the burning of Protestant diehards. The first to die, John Rogers (?1500-55), Vicar of Holy Sepulchre, Newgate perished at Smithfield in front of his wife and eleven children. A granite slab commemorates his agonies. The largest number of Mary's victims at a single location, thirteen, perished at Stratford, where there is a Victorian Gothic column to their memory. The sufferings of all three hundred who died for their faith were subsequently chronicled in John Foxe's *Book of Martyrs* which became, after the Bible, the most widely owned book in England. Ironically Mary did more than any other single individual to make England Protestant.

In 1557, to Mary's great joy, Philip returned briefly to the wife whom he had abandoned fourteen months after their wedding. Mary was

Piety, Power and Peril

The archetype of the new man of Renaissance England, Thomas More (1478-1535) was an accomplished student of Greek and Latin but rejected an academic or ecclesiastical career in favour of a legal one. A Londoner by birth, More was educated at the then best school in the City, St. Anthony's in Threadneedle Street. From there he went to Lambeth Palace as a protégé of Cardinal Morton, Archbishop of Canterbury, then studied at Oxford and after that qualified as a barrister at Lincoln's Inn.

More was initially attracted to the contemplative life and spent lengthy periods at the Charterhouse, subjecting himself to the monastic discipline of an order renowned for its resistance to the laxity which had become all too common among other religious houses in London. More also lectured on the theme of 'The City of God' at St. Lawrence Jewry, near his home in Bucklersbury. A stained-glass window now commemorates his association with the church. During these years More accumulated a circle of cultured friends including the royal physician Thomas Linacre, the classicist William Lily, the preacher John Colet, founder of St. Paul's School and the Dutch scholar Desiderius Erasmus, the foremost European intellect of his day. More himself would become a patron of Hans Holbein, who painted the celebrated group portrait of More with his family. A large-scale copy of this can be seen in the National Portrait Gallery, a miniature version in the British Galleries of the Victoria and Albert Museum.

First elected to parliament in 1504, in 1509 More represented Westminster and became a JP. In 1510 he became the City of London's Under-Sheriff. Despite the burden of his public and civic duties, the conduct of a busy City legal practice and the responsibilities of a numerous household, More also began to develop a literary career. His first significant prose work (1513-14) was a history of Richard III which contributed significantly to blackening that monarch's reputation and revealed More's awareness of the tensions between politics and principle. By 1515 More had attracted sufficient attention to be entrusted with the conduct of a commercial and diplomatic embassy to the Low Countries where, during hours of enforced idleness, he began the composition of the work that made him famous throughout Europe.

Utopia – Greek for 'No Place' – is a satirical fantasy which created a new genre of social critique. At one level it is a sharp expose of the crass materialism, corruption and shallowness of contemporary society; at another it is an indirect defence of Christian orthodoxy. The inhabitants of the 'ideal' society of Utopia are governed by pure reason and tolerate neither hunger nor homelessness but, without the blessing of revelation, are still content to institutionalise slavery.

Whatever More's intention in writing the book – still a matter of scholarly debate – it got him noticed. More was invited to join the king's council. In 1517 he played a prominent part in helping to suppress the xenophobic riots of 'Evil May Day'. In 1520 he was part of the royal entourage when Henry VIII met Francis I at the Field of the Cloth of Gold and was knighted the following year. In 1523 More served successfully as Speaker of the House of Commons and by 1525 had been raised to Chancellor of the Duchy of Lancaster.

More assisted Henry VIII in composing his attack on the teachings of Martin Luther, the *Defence of the Seven Sacraments*, which gained the king the papal title of 'Defender of the Faith'. More himself wrote bitter denunciations of Protestant teachings and also of William Tyndale, who was translating the Bible into English. With his *Dialogue Concerning Heresies* (1528) More began for the first time to aim at a wider readership by publishing in English.

Following Wolsey's disgrace and fall in 1529 More, although known to be opposed to the

22. *Sir Thomas More.*

23. *The statue of Sir Thomas More outside Chelsea Old Church.*

king's determination to annul his marriage to Catherine of Aragon, was pressed to take the Cardinal's place as Lord Chancellor. As the monarch's chief minister More directed his energies to legal reform and the punishment of recalcitrant heretics but his failure to contribute to resolving 'The King's Great Matter' led to his inevitable marginalisation. In 1532, after the English church surrendered its right to legislate for itself by acknowledging royal supremacy over its governance, More resigned his post and devoted himself to devotional writing. Arrested in 1534, he continued to write in the Tower, analogising Christ's suffering with his own torment and stoutly refusing either to endorse – or openly to deny - royal supremacy over the church. Incarcerated in the ancient Bell Tower, the ageing More was enfeebled by a wretched diet and inadequate clothing and finally denied even the refuge of books and writing materials. Unable to break down either More's deafening silence or the defiance it proclaimed, the king finally had

him convicted of treason on perjured evidence and executed at Tower Hill. More met his end with measured resolution, proclaiming that he died the King's good servant but God's first.

More's statue at Cheyne Walk was unveiled in 1969, outside Chelsea Old Church, where he himself had sung in the choir when living at his riverside retreat nearby. The Lord Chancellor's chain of office draped across his knees symbolises his renunciation of power in favour of principle. Another statue of More, curiously placed at first floor level, can be seen on the south-east corner of Lincoln's Inn, overlooking the rear of the Royal Courts of Justice. Sir Thomas More was beatified in 1886 and canonized in 1935. The 1967 film version of Robert Bolt's play *A Man For All Seasons* made More's story known to the wider world, with Paul Scofield playing a More of humour and humility, perhaps at the expense of the real man's harsher side. In 2000 Pope John Paul II proclaimed Saint Thomas More the patron saint of politicians.

induced to support a Spanish campaign in France, which resulted in the loss of Calais and its surrounding territory, the last English possession in that country. She never saw Philip again. She deluded herself into thinking she was pregnant – but she was dying.

Elizabeth (reigned 1558-1603)

Elizabeth I ruled by bullying her ministers and flattering her subjects. Vain, imperious, foul-tempered and foul-mouthed, she was completely devoted to the service and greatness of her realm. Both her ministers and her people knew it and adored her as 'Good Queen Bess'.

Elizabeth's accession was greeted joyously in London. An auspicious date for her coronation was selected in consultation with her magus Dr. John Dee (1527-1608). Despite the fact that Henry VIII had executed her mother, she reverenced his memory and the aura of majesty he had embodied. Like him the queen was musically gifted, a passionate hunter and even more ferociously clever. Elizabeth eventually spoke seven, possibly nine, languages and packed her court with learned men as well as brave and handsome ones.

Elizabeth lost no time in reclaiming her religious authority; but whereas her father claimed to be Head of the Church in England Elizabeth asserted herself as 'Supreme Governor' of the Church *of* England. The compromise which became Anglicanism combined a Protestant theology which distanced it from the 'old faith' with a style of worship still too like it to satisfy the reformists known as puritans. Once the queen had been excommunicated by the Pope in 1570 she became a permanent target for would-be suicide assassins. Sir Francis Walsingham (?1532-90) made it his personal mission in life to protect the queen from all plots and created Europe's first truly professional security and intelligence service to achieve this, inaugurating London's long history as a centre of unending espionage.

Although Elizabeth's government executed more people over the course of her reign than Mary had, that reign was nine times as long and

24. Elizabeth I; oil by Zucchero

executions were ordered on a case by case basis, not as a matter of general policy. She also strove to avoid outright war until it was forced on her. The destruction of the mighty Spanish Armada in 1588 was taken as a vindication of her rule by divine intervention and celebrated with immense pomp in St. Paul's. Not a single Spaniard landed on English soil. Not a single English ship was lost.

The closing decade of Elizabeth's reign was overshadowed with troubles and failures. Three successive seasons of disastrous weather brought the country to the brink of famine. Elizabeth's favourite, Robert Devereux, Earl of Essex (1566-1601), failed disastrously to suppress an Irish rebellion and then attempted a lunatic *putsch* in London, forcing the queen to order his execution. Elizabeth, however, remained resolute and resourceful to the end. In 1601, faced with a fractious Parliament, she disarmed them completely with what passed into legend as the 'Golden Speech', assuring the men from distant shires "Though God hath

25. *Sir Francis Walsingham, Queen Elizabeth's chief of security and intelligence. Oil, c.1584, attributed to John De Critz the Elder.*

26. *Robert Devereux, 2nd Earl of Essex.*

raised me high, yet this I count the glory of my crown: that I have reigned with your loves …". Elizabeth I died at Richmond aged sixty-nine, England's oldest sovereign to date.

Elizabeth spent little on building, content that others should bankrupt themselves creating 'prodigy houses' in which to entertain her and her court. Buried in Westminster Abbey in the same tomb as her half-sister Mary, Elizabeth's only memorial in London is a puppet-like statue, Byzantine in its stiffness, now in the courtyard of St. Dunstan-in-the-West, which once stood above Ludgate. Yet for two hundred years after her death the day of Elizabeth I's accession was still being celebrated as a public holiday.

CHAPTER THREE

Crisis and Constitutionalism

The Ultimate Terrorist Plot

Although himself a firm Protestant, James I (reigned 1603-25) was the son of an extravagantly devout Catholic, Mary Queen of Scots. Soon after acceding to the English throne James discreetly relaxed ferocious penal laws subjecting Catholics to the risk of fines, imprisonment and death. A vociferous Parliamentary uproar led to a rapid royal U-turn, leaving Catholics with a sense of betrayal.

The conclusion of peace with Spain in 1604 compounded this by depriving them of the hope of foreign help. A band of young Catholic conspirators, led by Robert Catesby (1572-1605) a wealthy, born-again zealot with a track record of activism, planned to use gunpowder to blow up Parliament while the king himself was in attendance, asserting, in Catesby's words, that "in that place have they done us all the mischief, and perchance God hath designed that place for

27. The execution of Gunpowder Plot conspirators at Westminster. in 1606.

37

in the words of one grateful admiral.

In 1672 Pepys was appointed Secretary to the Admiralty, enabling him to programme major reforms. His personal loyalty to the Roman Catholic James, Duke of York, Lord High Admiral and heir presumptive, rendered him, however, vulnerable to malicious charges of Popish sympathies, leading to his brief confinement in the Tower in 1680. Reappointed in 1684, Pepys's career was prematurely curtailed with James's deposition in 1688.

A keen musician and bibliophile, Pepys also served as Master of Trinity House, Master of the Clothworkers' Company, a Governor of Christ's Hospital and President of the Royal Society. A bust of Pepys stands in Seething Lane, near his former home and office. He lies opposite in St. Olave's, Hart Street where once he worshipped. A striking bust of his long-suffering spouse, Elizabeth, gazes down on his former pew. The portrait for which he paid £14 can be seen in the National Portrait Gallery. Appropriately for a man who did a great deal of business in public houses, Pepys is commemorated in the names of pubs in Mayfair, Vintry and Hackney. A museum of Pepyseana is in Prince Henry's Room on Fleet Street.

The Aroma of Intrigue

London's first coffee house was opened in St. Michael's Alley, off Cornhill in 1652. By the end of the century London had at least five hundred. The coffee-houses clustered in the City served primarily the purposes of their commercial clientele. Those around Fleet Street and Covent Garden were the gathering-place of wits, scholars, poets, lawyers, hacks and the printers and publishers who gave them intermittent employment. The coffee-houses of the capital's political epicentre, Westminster and St. James's became the haunt of factions. The British in Cockspur Street was home to outsiders whose abilities should have made them insiders but for the fact that they were not paid-up Anglicans – Dissenters, Scotsmen and the occasional colonial, like Benjamin Franklin. Army and Navy officers favoured the St. James's, also a stronghold

for supporters of the Whig party. Tories frequented Ozinda's or the Cocoa Tree in Pall Mall, which would in the eighteenth century be rumoured to serve as an informal rendezvous for Jacobites.

In December 1675 Charles II was persuaded that coffee-houses were breeding-grounds of sedition and intrigue and rashly ordered their wholesale closure:-

> "Whereas it is most apparent, That the Multitude of Coffee-houses of late Years set up ... and the great resort of Idle and Disaffected persons to them, have produced very evil and dangerous Effects ... for that in such Houses and by occasion of the meetings of such Persons therein, divers false, malicious and scandalous Reports are devised and spread abroad, to the Defamation of His Majesty's Government and to the Disturbance of the Peace and Quiet of the Realm; His Majesty hath thought it fit and necessary that the said Coffee-houses be Put down and Suppressed ...".

Such was the reaction to this proposal that the authorities moderated their demand for closure within ten days and postponed its implementation for six months. Eventually they settled for making coffee-house owners swear an Oath of Allegiance and "to be wonderful good for the future and to take care to suppress treasonable talk in their houses".

Continental visitors frequently remarked on the role of the coffee-houses as "the chief organs through which the public opinion of the metropolis vented itself", giving demonstrable daily proof of the extraordinary freedom of expression that Englishmen were beginning to claim as of right. This opinion has been endorsed by the cultural historian, Professor John Brewer:

> "They ... undermined the hierachical values of monarchical absolutism centred on the court; they encouraged a polyphony of public conversations which challenged the voice of the crown ... and they usurped the prerogative of the prince by debating politics, religion and literature.

34. 'Coffee House Politicians' c. 1733.

The coffee house ... thrived as a transmitter, spreading news from abroad and, as a receiver, depending on the intelligence of its customers and newsprint. It breathed the oxygen of publicity and this was precisely why the royal authorities disliked it."

The German cultural theorist Jurgen Habermas likewise identified the coffee-house as a crucial institution in the construction of what he dubbed "the public sphere", an open arena for the rational and critical discussion of contested contemporary issues. According to Habermas " a public sphere that functioned in

35. Sir Francis Bacon. Detail from oil by John Vanderbank (c.1731) after painting by unknown artist c.1618.

36. Thomas Hobbes. Engraving after Casper by Hollar.

the political realm arose first in Great Britain at the turn of the eighteenth century". Cambridge literary critic Terry Eagleton has delineated Habermas's construct in the following terms – "Poised between state and civil society, this bourgeois 'public sphere' … comprises a realm of social institutions – clubs, journals, coffee houses, periodicals – in which private individuals assemble for the free, equal interchange of reasonable discourse, thus welding themselves into a relatively cohesive body whose deliberations may assume the form of a powerful political force." When the Croatian immigrant Pasqua Rosee opened that first London coffee-house back in 1652 he can have had little notion of just what he had started.

Intellectual Insiders

Bacon, Hobbes, Milton and Locke are conventionally thought of as literary or philosophical giants of their day; but each was also a political figure, though contrasting in their degrees of engagement or detachment.

A Gray's Inn man for forty-nine years, **Francis**

Bacon (1561-1626), a nephew of Elizabeth I's most trusted counsellor, William Cecil, was an M.P. by the age of twenty-three. He consolidated his public position by prosecuting his former patron, the Earl of Essex and later did the same for another fallen favourite, Raleigh. Bacon himself found favour with James I, who promoted him meteorically through the ranks of the legal profession to its summit as Lord Chancellor. In 1621, however, Bacon was convicted, on his own confession, of taking bribes, a relatively pardonable failing one would have thought in an age when virtually everyone did. And Bacon was relatively pardoned, suffering only a token spell in the Tower and the loss of his birthplace, York House in the Strand, to the king's egregious favourite, the Duke of Buckingham. Best known for his pithy *Essays* and his exposition of the potential of science, Bacon also bequeathed a utopian vision in his posthumously published *New Atlantis* (1627), which recast the Platonic ideal of the philosopher-king to envisage a Pacific island governed by 'Solomon's House', an academy of sciences dedicated to an endless

37. *John Milton. Oil by Van der Gucht.*

38. *John Locke, by Godfrey Kneller.*

quest for "the knowledge of causes and secret motions of things; and the enlarging the bounds of human empire, to the effecting of all things possible".

Thomas Hobbes (1588-1679) lived close to power but never attempted to exercise it himself. Tutor and secretary to the wealthy and influential Cavendish family, Earls of Devonshire, he also taught mathematics to the future Charles II and was a friend of Bacon. Hobbes sat out the civil wars in Paris, working on his magnum opus, *Leviathan, or the Matter, Form and Power of a Commonwealth, Ecclesiastical and Civil.* Unlike Aristotle, whom he had held in contempt since his Oxford days, Hobbes saw man not as an innately social being but as essentially selfish and potentially violent but capable of restraint through an appeal to his rationality. The 'State of Nature', far from being a paradise from which Man had excluded himself by the artificialities of civilization, was rather one of a war of all against all, justice an irrelevance, fear ubiquitous and "the life of man solitary, poor, nasty, brutish and short". Social peace, in Hobbes's bleak

view, was to be obtained by covenants ruthlessly enforced by a sovereign power, whether a single ruler or an assembly, to which even the church must be subordinate. The sovereign power to be sovereign must be indivisible – but when it ceases to protect it also ceases to command allegiance. Hobbes' radical realism saw him accused of justifying both atheism and absolutism. Charles II nevertheless gave him a pension – and bade him publish no more.

Educated at St. Paul's and Christ's College, Cambridge and self-educated in Italy, **John Milton** (1608-74), dithering between poetry and the ministry, seemed destined to become an eternal student until an inopportune marriage led him to publish a pamphlet on the desirability of divorce and another, attacking episcopacy, brought him to public attention. In 1644 he published *Areopagitica: a speech of Mr. John Milton for the liberty of unlicenc'd printing, to the Parliament of England.* Steeped in the classics, Milton took his title from the Areopagus, the meeting-place of the Athenian Upper Council, near the

Acropolis. Inspired at least partly by Parliament's efforts to suppress his pamphlet on divorce, Milton denounced censorship as a favoured instrument of those Puritan and English bugbears, the Papacy and the Inquisition, and praised diversity of opinion as the true guarantor of the growth of knowledge. The clinching argument is an appeal to national vanity as the "Lords and Commons of England" are bidden to consider "what Nation it is whereof ye are governors; A Nation not slow and dull, but of a quick, ingenious and piercing spirit ... a noble and puissant nation rousing herself like a strong man after sleep and shaking her invincible locks ...".

In 1649, following the execution of Charles I, Milton produced an exculpatory rationale in *The Tenure of Kings and Magistrates* which argued that a people "free by nature" had the inherent right to depose tyrants. Appointed Latin Secretary to the Council of State, Milton continued in that office despite the fact that he was almost totally blind by 1652. During the interregnum following Cromwell's death he published a rallying-cry for the republican cause *The Ready and Easy Way to Establish a Free Commonwealth*. Fleeing into hiding at the Restoration, Milton was arrested, fined and released to take refuge in the obscurity of Bunhill Row and the composition of his religious masterpieces *Paradise Lost* and *Paradise Regained*, epic expositions of the politics of Heaven and Hell.

John Locke (1632-1704) was educated at Westminster School. As an academic at Christ Church, Oxford from 1652 to 1667 he dabbled in law and medicine, wrote poetry and produced religious tracts. Locke was then taken up by the ambitious Earl of Shaftesbury and brought to live at Exeter House in the Strand as his family physician and intellectual factotum. Elected a Fellow of the Royal Society in 1668, from 1672 to 1675 Locke served as Secretary to the Council of Trade and Plantations, in which capacity he drafted a constitution for the Carolinas which included a guarantee of religious toleration. After living in France (1675-9), Locke returned to London (1679-83) until Shaftesbury's leading role in trying to get James II excluded from the succession to the throne forced him, and Locke as his protégé, to flee to the Netherlands. The 'Glorious Revolution' which brought about the overthrow of James II, the installation of William and Mary and the definitive establishment of the supremacy of Parliament over the throne enabled Locke to return from exile and live in Westminster. Nevertheless his *Two Treatises on Government*, arguing the basically contractual nature of legitimate rule, appeared anonymously in 1689. Locke's *Letter Concerning Toleration* argued that religious conviction was a matter of individual conscience, that churches are by nature voluntary associations and that therefore neither is coercion to be practised nor uniformity sought – a liberal posture somewhat vitiated by Locke's unwillingness to embrace either atheists or Catholics within his dispensation. Locke's classic defence of liberty and property was to exert the most profound influence on the drafters of the constitution of the United States.

Custom, Its power

"The predominance of custom is every where visible ... We see also the reign or tyranny of custom ... Therefore, since custom is the principal magistrate of man's life, let men by all means endeavour to obtain good customs. Certainly, custom is most perfect when it beginneth in young years: this we call education ... if the force of custom simply and separate be great, the force of custom copulate and conjoined and collegiate is far greater. For there example teacheth, company comforteth, emulation quickeneth, glory raiseth; so as in such places the force of custom is in his exaltation. Certainly, the great multiplication of virtues upon human nature resteth upon societies well ordained and disciplined. For commonwealths and governments do nourish virtue grown, but do not much mend the seed."

Francis Bacon *Essays*

CHAPTER FOUR

From Revolution to Revolution

Palace and Parliament

Dying without legitimate issue, Charles II nevertheless managed to outmanoeuvre the efforts of the Earl of Shaftesbury *(see p. 50)* and the embryonic Whig party and assure the succession of his Catholic convert brother as James II. James's reign (1685-88) was too brief to have any substantial impact on London but it had an immense impact on the constitution.

A stubborn man, James started as he meant to continue, having himself privately crowned and anointed in his Catholic chapel in Whitehall before going through the motions of an Anglican coronation at the Abbey the following day, April 23rd – St. George's Day. In June the late king's eldest illegitimate son, the handsome and popular but devious and dim, James Scott, Duke of Monmouth (1649-85), attempted an insurrection in the West Country in the Protestant cause. This was easily crushed in the last battle fought on English soil, at Sedgemoor. Monmouth was despatched at Tower Hill in one of the most famously botched executions in its long and bloody history.

When James issued a Declaration of Indulgence for the benefit of non-Anglicans seven bishops who protested were imprisoned in the Tower but then acquitted of seditious libel. In the same month, June 1688, the queen gave birth at St. James's Palace to a son, which meant that, instead of passing to James's Protestant daughters, Mary (1662-94) and Anne (1665-1714), the throne would pass on his death to a Catholic male. At the invitation of a cabal of seven Whig Protestant grandees Mary's husband, William, Prince of Orange (1650-1702), mounted a full-scale but unopposed invasion. William's motley force included Dutch, Danes, Huguenots and even Finns. British troops were ordered to withdraw from London to avoid the possibility of confrontation. Thus was the revolution rendered bloodless and therefore in retrospect 'Glorious'. Deserted by his own army, thanks largely to officer defections organised by the future Duke of Marlborough *(see p. 52)*, James fled into exile, sealing his fate when an attempted counter-coup in Ireland was defeated at the battle of the Boyne by the new 'King Billy'.

William and Mary were offered the throne in the Banqueting House, crowned and ruled jointly. The condition of their rule was the passage through Parliament of a Bill of Rights defining the limits of royal power and a Mutiny Act which required annual renewal, thus guaranteeing the impossibility of monarchical rule without Parliament.

William, a chronic asthmatic, refused to live in the palace of Whitehall and had Kensington House hastily converted to become the favoured royal residence. In 1698 Whitehall was utterly devastated by an accidental fire, although the Banqueting House was saved.

Mary died of smallpox at Kensington in 1694. William, Duke of Gloucester, the only surviving child of William's sister-in-law, Anne, died in 1700. Given William's refusal to remarry and Anne's track record of miscarriages and stillbirths, Parliament assured the continuity of a Protestant succession by the Act of Settlement of 1701, which decreed that, after Anne, the crown should pass to the House of Hanover.

Pint-sized, hook-nosed William was disliked for his Dutch favourites and his severe manner but his marriage to the statuesque, handsome Mary became an adoring partnership. William's acceptance of a foreign throne enabled him to harness British resources in support of his political life's purpose – checking the hegemony of France. One enduring side-effect of the king's wars was the foundation of the Bank of England in 1694 to finance them.

The equestrian statue of William III by John Bacon the Younger in St. James's Square *(see p. 150)* was placed there in 1808. William is depicted as a Roman general. Under the hooves of his horse is a molehill, a reminder of the hazard which caused his fatal riding-accident and led generations of Jacobites to toast the "little gentleman in black velvet". The statue of William III outside Kensington Palace, by Heinrick Baucke, was presented "for the British nation" in 1907 by Kaiser Wilhelm II – doubtless as a dig at his Francophile uncle, Edward VII.

Dull but Dutiful

Walter Bagehot *(see p. 95)* said of Queen Anne, that never was so small a person set in so great a place.

Anne's unlikely destiny was to preside over the succession of dazzling victories laid at her feet by her great captain John Churchill, Duke of Marlborough (1650-1722), whose wife, Sarah, was the queen's closest confidante. In 1707, when the Act of Union abolished Scotland's separate parliament in return for a disproportionate Scottish representation at Westminster, Anne's title was changed from 'Queen of England, Scotland, France and Ireland' to 'Queen of Great Britain, France and Ireland'.

Diminutive, devout, kindly but unintellectual, Anne was broken in health by seventeen pregnancies, rheumatism and chronic gout by the time she even ascended the throne. Excessive eating and drinking would eventually inflate her to twenty stones. Perhaps the queen's own poor health encouraged her to reintroduce the custom of touching for the 'King's Evil' (scrofula) William had rejected with undisguised contempt.

Although Anne was quick to put Handel under court patronage she was indifferent to the arts, preferring gambling at cards and stag-hunting. Sincere devotion to the Anglican church made her an enthusiastic supporter of the 'Bluecoat'

39. Queen Anne's statue outside St Paul's Cathedral.

charity schools established throughout London by the Society for the Promotion of Christian Knowledge. The same alarm at the expansion of Nonconformist sects which had inspired this initiative won her warm endorsement for the Act of 1711, which granted a million pounds for the construction of fifty new Anglican churches throughout the capital. The pledge was never fulfilled but the generous, indeed elastic, budgets did permit the construction of such landmarks as Thomas Archer's St. John's, Smith Square and Hawksmoor's East End masterpieces, St. George's-in-the-East, St. Anne's, Limehouse and Christ Church, Spitalfields. From her own resources the monarch established Queen Anne's Bounty to increase the stipends of poorer clergy and build and repair parsonage houses.

The statue of Queen Anne which stands in front of St. Paul's cathedral was originally erected in 1712 to celebrate the completion of Wren's masterpiece. Sculpted by Francis Bird, the statue decayed badly and was replaced in 1886 by a sub-standard copy which still flatters the corpulent monarch. Another statue by Bird adorns the Market Hall of Kingston-on-Thames.

40. *The masthead of the first edition of The Times (previously the Daily Universal Register) in 1788.*

Fit To Print

In 1695 the Licensing Act passed in 1662 was allowed to lapse, leading to the establishment of a number of news-sheets which appeared three times a week. Their titles – *Post Boy*, *Post Man* and *Flying Post* – underline their essential purpose to relay information to eager readers who were not in London – or at least not in the appropriate circles in London – to be privy to the latest political chit-chat in person. The first daily imprint, the *Daily Courant*, appeared in 1702 and lasted until 1735. By 1760 there were four London dailies and by 1790 fourteen. The first Sunday newspaper, the *Sunday Monitor*, was published in 1779 and joined by the *Observer* in 1791. *The Times* first appeared in 1785 as the *Daily Universal Register*, changing its name in 1788.

A Stamp Duty, introduced in 1715 to make sure that papers remained expensive enough to be confined to the educated classes, brought in £911 in its first year; by 1781 the expansion of the press meant that it was yielding over £40,000. By the 1770s Parliament abandoned its rearguard action to suppress reporting of its debates. Readership was considerably higher than limited print-runs would imply as the less wealthy could peruse the press in coffee-houses, taverns and barber shops.

Dull Dynasty

Under the rule of the House of Hanover kings were increasingly stripped of their constitutional powers but, in a century of more or less constant warfare, remained a rallying-point for national loyalty. Linda Colley has stressed the emergence under Hanoverian rule of a truly British identity, forged through the interaction of armed conflict, imperial expansion and a fierce Protestantism, which united the political elite in particular as an Anglo-Scottish-Irish aristocracy of adventurers, globally on the make. The prominence achieved in London by such Scotsmen as Lord Mansfield and Adam Smith or such Irishmen as Edmund Burke and R.B. Sheridan underlines her point. Although Edinburgh was to be rebuilt as 'the Athens of the North' and Dublin was transformed into a great and gracious city, inevitably all of the greatest talents of the age were drawn to London.

As a dynasty the Hanoverian kings and their offspring were healthy, highly sexed, self-indulgent, physically brave, inclined to corpulence, lovers of country sports and music rather than literature, viciously quarrelsome and sticklers for etiquette and routine. Preferring domestic life to public display, they built no new palaces, preferring to adapt or upgrade existing ones. As a contemporary foreigner perceptively remarked, while English dukes lived like kings, English kings were content to live like dukes.

George I (reigned 1714-27)

George I succeeded to the throne under the terms of the Act of Settlement after fifty other claimants with a better claim by blood, thanks to the fact that he was a Protestant and none of them were.

attracted the attendance of politicians out of favour under the current regime. George II's relationship with his son, Frederick Prince of Wales (1707-51), proved to be one of mutual contempt and antagonism. Although brought up at arm's length in Hanover 'Fred' anglicised with a will to become a devotee of dog-fighting and drunkenness. Denounced by his parents as "a liar and a beast", the heir presumptive died after being struck by the ball during a cricket match.

George II had an encyclopaedic memory for the minutiae of military life and achieved worthwhile reforms in the administration of the army, eliminating much peculation, standardising drill systems and introducing a numbered system of regimental organisation. He also established the ceremony of Trooping the Colour and the daily ritual of Changing the Guard. In 1743 at the battle of Dettingen he became, at the age of sixty, the last king of Britain to lead his troops in person. After his horse bolted to the rear of the battle line he ran back through the ranks to harangue his soldiers – "Now boys, fire and be brave and the French will soon run." Which they did.

In 1745 the rebel Jacobite army of 'Bonnie Prince Charlie' (1720-88) took Carlisle and Newcastle and got as far south as Derby, throwing all London in a panic. George despatched his own son the brutal Duke of – 'Butcher' – Cumberland (1721-65) to command the Anglo-Scottish army which annihilated the Highlanders in the last battle fought on British soil, at Culloden, in 1746. In celebration of the salvation of the dynasty Thomas Arne wrote *God Save Great George Our King*, which became the world's first national anthem.

George II became the last king to be buried in Westminster Abbey. Although it was more than twenty years since the death of his wife of thirty-two years George ordered that the side of his coffin should be broken that his dust might mingle with hers. Courtly and courteous, he may have been underrated by historians because, working through the spoken word and terse written annotations to documents, he left little personal documentation from which to assess the exercise of his undoubted influence over affairs and appointments. There is a statue of George II by van Nost in Golden Square, Soho, another at Greenwich Hospital by Michael Rysbrack and excellent terra cotta busts of the king and his queen by the same sculptor in Kensington Palace. The American state of Georgia, founded in 1732 as a reformatory for London's minor offenders and debtors, was named in the king's honour. Augusta, Georgia was named for Fred's widow, the Princess of Wales who was chiefly responsible for the development of the Royal Botanic Gardens at Kew.

George III (reigned 1760-1820)

The premature death of Fred meant that on George II's death the throne passed to his grandson as George III. Born prematurely at Norfolk House in St. James's Square *(see p. 150)*, he ascended the throne at an apogee of national success, following a string of brilliant victories over France and her allies in the Seven Years War (1756-63). George was the first British monarch to study science and was tutored in drawing, architecture and music. Capable of speaking German, French and Latin, the king spoke English as his native language and proclaimed to his first Parliament "I glory in the name of Briton". He never visited Hanover. Ill-advised by Lord Bute, his former tutor, who became his first prime minister, the king surrendered numerous traditional sources of royal income in return for a consolidated Civil List which, despite a lifestyle which was positively frugal by Continental standards, proved too niggardly, plaguing him with financial problems throughout his reign. Unlike his predecessors the king was a model of fidelity to his consort, Charlotte of Mecklenburgh-Strelitz (1744-1818), whom he had married sight unseen. They had fifteen children. Treating his official residence, St. James's Palace, as a place of work, the king bought nearby Buckingham House as a domestic refuge where he could enjoy the company of his family. It accordingly became

King Mob

The word 'mob', a contraction of the Latin *mobile vulgus* ('inconstant crowd') was first recorded in that year of political excitement, 1688. Swift deplored the neologism and insisted that the correct term was 'rabble'. Modern usage associates that term with the lowest levels of the social order. The patient researches of Professor George Rudé, however, established that the rioting mobs which became so celebrated a feature of eighteenth-century London could be drawn from a much broader cross-section of its population, including not only ruffians, casual labourers and apprentices, but also on occasion, skilled artisans and even petty businessmen. Rudé concluded that "it is ... a surprising fact that the most riotous parts of London ... were not the crowded quarters of St. Giles in the Fields or the shadier alleys of Holborn but the more solid and respectable popular districts of the City, the Strand, Southwark, Shoreditch and Spitalfields."

Rioting was a general resort of the voteless throughout Britain, usually protesting at food prices, enclosures, turnpikes, workhouses, militia service or crackdowns on smuggling. London was different in a number of ways. Food riots were virtually unknown. But the sheer size and diversity of the city meant that almost anything else might spark off a riot thanks to the relative ease of assembling a self-selected quorum of the aggrieved. There was also a greater propensity for riots to become politicised by association with a party, faction or interest. In the course of the eighteenth century Londoners would riot against dissenting chapels, the attempted imposition of an Excise, attempts to curb sales of gin, the employment of cheap immigrant Irish labour, performances by French actors, the naturalization of Jews, the importation of Indian cottons and French silks, the importation of foreign technology in the silk industry, theatre admission prices and the relief of Roman Catholic disabilities. They also rioted in favour of higher wages, the ruling house of Hanover, war with Spain, Pitt the Elder and John Wilkes *(see p. 65).*

(see p. 65).

The anti-Catholic Gordon Riots of 1780 were the largest popular disturbances ever to occur in the entire history of London. Widespread anti-Catholic feeling was fed by Britain's recurrent wars against the Catholic great powers of Europe, France and Spain, by lingering hostility to the Jacobite cause and by more immediate hostility to the growing number of the capital's Irish population, whose willingness to work for low wages was much resented. Sympathy for Catholics, on the other hand, was present among sections of the political elite, who realised that Jacobitism was dead, deplored religious bigotry on intellectual grounds, were certainly not competing for work with Irish labourers and, more cynically, recognised that the recruitment of Catholic Highlanders might greatly assist an army already hard-pressed by American rebels in the colonies.

Popular reaction to parliamentary proposals for easing the laws which discriminated against Catholics was energised by a Protestant Association headed by a youthful MP, the mentally unstable Lord George Gordon (1751-93). On 2nd June 1780 a massive crowd, estimated at 60,000 gathered in St. George's Fields, Lambeth to march on Parliament, ostensibly to present a monster petition against further measures to relieve Catholics of their civil disadvantages. Such an immense crowd soon proved far beyond control, let alone co-ordination, by its nominal leader. The preliminary targets of what rapidly became a mob were suspected Catholic sympathisers in the House of Lords, several of whom were singled out and roughed up. This was followed by attacks on the chapels attached to the embassies of Sardinia and Bavaria. Technically these were only for the use of diplomatic staff but in practice, staffed by Irish priests, they were largely attended by members of London's 14,000-strong Catholic population. The homes of alleged Catholic sympathisers

47. Hogarth's 'March to Finchley' depicting the British army as an undisciplined rabble. They are at the junction of today's Euston Road and Tottenham Court Road.

repeal of a recent Act of Parliament to enhance the civil liberties enjoyed by Britain's Jewish community.

Hogarth's social conscience made him a governor of St. Bartholomew's Hospital and a generous supporter of London's and England's first orphanage, the Foundling Hospital in Bloomsbury. Hogarth's political *nous* secured the passage of the Copyright Act of 1735 which for the first time gave legal protection to the rights of visual artists, in the way that writers had long enjoyed.

Big City, Small Government

London's population passed the half million mark by the beginning of the eighteenth century,

making it the third city of Europe, after Paris and Naples. Reconstruction of the ancient City after the Great Fire of 1666 had lowered its population density and adorned it with a new Royal Exchange, dozens of handsome churches and, in Wren's St. Paul's, a cathedral second only in size and grandeur to St. Peter's in Rome. There had, however, been no corresponding overhaul in London's institutions, which continued to grow in complexity rather than competence. The Mayor and Corporation of the City of London exercised their authority through no less than seventeen courts, with a range of administrative, electoral, legislative and judicial functions, plus some one-hundred and fifty officials, many of whose offices were, however, mere sinecures to be bought and sold for the benefit of their holders. The City also governed the bailiwick of Southwark, though not its neighbouring parishes, which were part of Surrey, and exercised several jurisdictions which went far beyond the immediate boundaries of the Square Mile, controlling markets over a radius of seven miles, levying coal duties over a radius of twelve miles and administering the Port of London and eighty miles of the River Thames. Westminster, home to Parliament, the Court, the courts, the machinery of central government and the residences of the two hundred or so politically active Lords and dozens of MPs, had no corporate status but was loosely administered by an unpaid Court of Burgesses and the magistrates of Middlesex. Areas that were becoming its residential extensions, such as Marylebone and St. Pancras were governed by their parish vestries, as was the rest of the metropolis, amounting to some two hundred by the end of the century. Just under half of these were 'closed' vestries, run by a self-perpetuating petty oligarchy, which frequently abused their powers and purse. The rest were 'open' and subject to some degree of electoral surveillance and the rotation of office-holders.

Despite London's lack of a unified governing authority a number of major projects were achieved, most notably the building of an imposing Mansion House, the construction of new bridges at Westminster and Blackfriars and the laying out of the capital's first by-pass, the New Road, now the Marylebone and Euston Roads. Central government initiatives added the Horse Guards, Admiralty, Somerset House and 10 Downing Street (*see p. 174*). In 1762 Westminster obtained an Act which inaugurated dramatic improvements in its paving, lighting and refuse-disposal arrangements, an initiative taken up in the City and elsewhere, but on a piecemeal basis which basically conferred such benefits on the better-off districts of the metropolis, if anything heightening the contrast between them and the slums and wastelands around and between them. Apart from the establishment of the celebrated Bow Street Runners to enforce magistrates' warrants and the belated establishment of a dedicated River Police unit, the machinery for the suppression of crime and maintenance of order remained quite inadequate for a city which continued to grow inexorably in both area and population.

In the unreformed House of Commons London as a whole, larger in population than the next fifty British cities added together, had fewer representatives than rural Wiltshire, far fewer than distant Cornwall. The City was represented by four M.P.s, elected by its freemen at a meeting of Common Hall. Westminster's two Members were chosen by an even larger electorate, thanks to rising property values, which enabled many petty tradesmen to qualify as forty-shilling freeholders. It was therefore singularly and unusually free of the landlord influence so dominant in most constituencies and thus at liberty to plump for maverick candidates like John Wilkes (*see p. 65*). The out-parishes of Middlesex and Surrey likewise had two MPs, also elected by forty-shilling freeholders.

The City was broadly, sometimes vociferously, supportive of the Hanoverian dynasty, although it also harboured some well-closeted Jacobites, even at the level of the mayoralty. At the time of Bonnie Prince Charlie's rising in 1745 the Mayor and Aldermen hastened to send an Address of Loyalty to the King and Common Council launched a Defence Fund with a donation of £1,000. Three hundred and fifty residents of the wealthy parish of St. George's, Hanover Square, where Tory generals were particularly thick on the ground, likewise pledged money for the capital's defence. A hundred and thirty-three master silk-weavers of Spitalfields, most of Huguenot descent, hastened to demonstrate their allegiance to Crown and country by promising a force of three thousand volunteers from among their "workmen, servants and dependants".

Attitudes towards the government of the day, by contrast, were frequently antagonistic, despite the fact that they needed each other. Governments needed City institutions like the Bank of England, the South Sea Company, the East India Company and the leading insurance offices, to subscribe to for forty-five guests. The government tried forcing Wilkes' expulsion from Parliament and instigating libel prosecutions in relation to the *North Briton* and an *Essay on Woman*, a pornographic satire on Pope's celebrated *Essay on Man*. Exchanges in the House led to a duel in which Wilkes was wounded. He then fled to Paris.

Eventually driven back by lack of funds, Wilkes returned from self-imposed exile in 1768 and succeeded in having himself returned as Member of Parliament for the county of Middlesex, which, unlike most eighteenth-century constituencies, had an unusually large electorate beyond the ready control of any magnate. Wilkes found a capable campaign manager in the person of Horne Tooke *(see below)*. Having made his political come-back, Wilkes surrendered himself to the Court of King's Bench and was imprisoned for two years. When boisterous supporters gathered outside the prison to hail their hero the troops despatched to disperse them fired on the crowd, inflicting fatalities. Wilkes' denunciation of the 'St. George's Field massacre' led Lord Grafton's government to have him expelled again from Parliament on grounds of libel. The electors of Middlesex responded by re-electing Wilkes three times in succession in three months, despite Parliament's repeated refusal to accept him. Once again cast in the role of the common man being victimised by an overbearing administration, Wilkes became the darling of the mob. Admirers, co-ordinated by Horne Tooke, formed a Society of Supporters of the Bill of Rights to champion the Wilkite cause.

Released in 1770, Wilkes was elected an Alderman of the City of London, then Sheriff and in 1774 became its Lord Mayor. In that same year he was again elected for Middlesex and at last took his seat. Although he remained a supporter of reformist causes and opposed military action against the American rebels he was no longer the darling of the mob and, indeed, helped to suppress it during the Gordon riots of 1780. By 1784 he had become a supporter of Pitt and a stranger to the radicals. The inscription on his coffin nonetheless proclaimed him 'A Friend of Liberty'.

John Wilkes liked to shock and often did but he could also charm. Despite his ugliness and a pronounced squint, he was a successful womanizer, boasting that it "took him only half an hour to talk away his face" Dr. Johnson, who thought him a thoroughly bad hat, was once tricked into dining in company with him and grudgingly found him to be both witty and well-informed. Edward Gibbon recorded that he had "scarcely ever met with a better companion, he has inexhaustible spirits, infinite wit and humour, and a great deal of knowledge; but a thorough profligate in principle as in practice, his life is stained with every vice, and his conversation full of blasphemy and indecency … shame is a weakness he has long since surmounted." Wilkes's wit was rapier fast. Invited to join in a hand of cards he once declined on the grounds that "I am so ignorant that I cannot tell the difference between a king and a knave." When Lord Sandwich predicted that he would die either of the pox or on the gallows Wilkes replied "That depends, my lord, whether I embrace your mistress or your principles." Horace Walpole judged Wilkes a mere political opportunist, guilty of a sort of political frivolousness which was careless of the interests or even the lives of those he affected to defend –

"wantonness, rather than ambition or vengeance, guided his hand; and though he became the martyr of the best cause, there was nothing in his principles or morals that led him to care under what government he lived. To laugh and riot and scatter fire-brands with him was liberty …"

A statue of John Wilkes, erected in 1988, stands in Fetter Lane. Cross-eyed and corpulent, he holds a copy of the 'Bill for the Just and Better Representation of the People of England' which he put before the Commons in 1776.

Devil's Advocate

John Horne Tooke (1736-1812) started out as an ordained minister and undertook the Grand Tour in the capacity of cicerone, meeting such luminaries as the great Voltaire. A fortunate inheritance enabled him to forsake the ministry for a life of abrasive activism. He also became

49. John Horne Tooke.

50. Thomas Paine, c.1876

renowned for hosting political suppers attended by intellects as varied as Bentham, Paine and Coleridge. In 1768 he took the lead in organizing John Wilkes' Westminster election campaign. When he tried to organize a fund for the relief of the Americans killed in the fracas at Lexington he was sent to prison for a year. In 1781 Tooke established the Society for Constitutional Information to press for parliamentary reform. In 1792 he helped to establish the London Corresponding Society, which sought to extend the franchise to the working classes, and in 1794 was acquitted of a charge of high treason for the role he had played in its activities. An immensely learned student of Anglo-Saxon and etymology, Tooke was passionately convinced that much political discourse was obfuscated or perverted by a simple failure to understand the true meanings of basic terms. Brougham thought Tooke crafty and manipulative, too distrusted ever to achieve much in terms of practical politics. Hazlitt concurred – "Provided he could say a clever or spiteful thing he did not care whether it served or injured the cause. Spleen or the exercise of intellectual power was the motive of his patriotism, rather than principle."

Revolutionary on Two Continents

Tom Paine (1737-1809) was born into a Norfolk Quaker family and passed the first half of his life uneventfully as a stay-maker and an excise officer. An attempt to negotiate a pay rise for excisemen got him branded as a trouble-maker and sacked. A chance meeting with Benjamin Franklin in London led Paine to emigrate to Pennsylvania in 1774. There Paine finally found his métier as a journalist. Paine's pamphlet *Common Sense* (1776), justifying the cause of American independence and the superiority of republican government, sold at least 150,000 copies in a matter of months and catapulted its author into the position of chief ideologist of the revolution. *Common Sense* impressed the Americans immensely. Paine also impressed himself –

" I have not only contributed to raise a new empire in the world, founded on a new system of government, but I arrived at an eminence in political literature, the most difficult of all lines to succeed and excel in, which aristocracy, with all its aids, has not been able to reach or rival."

Paine served as secretary to the Committee for Foreign Affairs and after the war was rewarded with a farm in New York. Returning to England in 1787 to pursue a bridge-building project, Paine became side-tracked by his enthusiasm for the French revolution and in a riposte to Burke's attack on it *(see p. 74)* rushed out *The Rights of Man* (1791) which ran through eight editions within the year. A second section, attacking monarchy, led to a charge of treason, forcing Paine to flee to France, where he was made an honorary citizen and elected to the National Convention before falling victim to the Terror and spending a year in prison, where he began *The Age of Reason*, an attack on orthodox religion. Convicted of treason in England in *absentia*, Paine was unable to return to his homeland and finally left France for the USA in 1802. A forgotten figure, if noticed only to be despised as an atheist – he was actually a Deist – Paine passed his last years in poverty, clouded by alcoholism. On his death the *New York Citizen* observed "He had lived long, did some good and much harm." When Paine's bones were repatriated to England a decade later by William Cobbett *(see below)* they were lost. A plaque and sculpture at Angel Square, Islington claims that Paine wrote *The Rights of Man* while staying there.

John Cartwright

Cartwright (1740-1824), by origin a Lincolnshire squire and a naval veteran of the Seven Years War, emerged in 1774 as one of the first English supporters of American ambitions for independence by publishing *American independence the Glory and Interest of Great Britain*. In 1775 Cartwright resigned his commission rather than fight the rebels in the American colonies. In the same year, however, he accepted the rank of major in the militia, a rank he

51. John Cartwright.

ultimately lost on account of his support for the French revolution. In the same year that Americans declared their independence Cartwright published *Take Your Choice* in which he set out what were to be the basic demands of parliamentary reformers for the next century – manhood suffrage, voting by secret ballot, equal electoral districts, the payment of MPs and annual elections. With Horne Tooke Cartwright was a co-founder in 1780 of the Society for Constitutional Information which soon, however, lost its way, becoming distracted by such causes as the anti-slavery movement, prison reform and the civic emancipation of Dissenters. Cartwright was also active in promoting the circulation of Paine's *Rights of Man* and in 1794 served as a defence witness for Horne Tooke. Cartwright's last major initiative was the establishment in 1812 of the Hampden Club to renew the campaign for parliamentary reform. Initially attractive to the gentry, Hampden Clubs were formed throughout the provinces, where they drew working-class support in sufficient strength for them to organise a national

52. Charles James Fox caricatured as the Greek orator Demosthenes.

IV of France, Fox was educated at Eton and Oxford, becoming an accomplished classicist. His indulgent father encouraged rather than curbed an extravagant and dissolute lifestyle in which heavy drinking, reckless gambling and irregular liaisons figured prominently. By the time he was 25 Fox had already run up debts of £140,000. A superb orator and conversationalist of dazzling charm and wit, Fox was only 19 when he entered the Commons. He consistently attacked the influence of the crown, supported the cause of the American colonists, championed the defence of civil liberties and supported a negotiated peace with France. Over the course of his last decade Fox finally began to stabilize at least his private life. Political friends once more paid off his debts and provided him with a comfortable income. He repaid them by giving up racing and gambling. He married his mistress. And, just before his demise, he finally managed one great achievement, moving the resolution which led to the abolition of the slave trade within the British Empire. A statue of Fox, by Sir Francis Chantrey, was erected in Bloomsbury Square just ten years after his death. Clad in a Roman toga in testimony of his eloquence, it depicts Fox clutching a scroll, anachronistically representing Magna Carta in token of his devotion to the cause of liberty and curbing the power of the crown. At the foot of Fox's monument in Westminster Abbey a sorrowing African slave mourns in gratitude. In Soho the name of a public house *The Intrepid Fox* recalls both his political courage and the fact that he once represented Westminster in Parliament. A blue plaque records Fox's former residence at 46 Clarges Street, Mayfair.

convention in 1817. This was deemed subversive by the government, leading to the suppression of the Hampden Club movement nationwide. Cartwright's statue shows him sitting in a chair with his back to the tennis-courts in Cartwright Gardens, Bloomsbury.

Charles James Fox

Born into a brilliant and wealthy aristocratic family **Charles James Fox** (1749-1806) made a career of political perverseness, conducting a lifelong vendetta against George III which virtually guaranteed his isolation in opposition. Craving office, he did serve twice as foreign secretary – the first in English history - but over the course of a lengthy public life exercised power for less than a year in total. As he correctly predicted of himself – "great reputation I think I may acquire and keep, great situation I never can acquire, nor if acquired, keep without making sacrifices I never will make." A descendant of Charles II of England and Henri

Utopians

Thomas Spence (1750-1814), originally a teacher in Newcastle, outlined a Utopian vision in his *The Real Rights of Man* (1775) which called for all land to be held in common by each parish, the rents it generated being used to support local administration, public libraries and schools. Parishes would also each select a representative for a national assembly. All adult males would

53. William Godwin; oil by James Northcote, 1802.

be obligated to serve in the militia. Moving to London in the 1787, Spence became a bookseller and an active member of the London Corresponding Society. Although by temperament much more the educator than the activist, Spence did allow members of a shadowy militant group to practise arms drill in a large room above his bookshop. He also began issuing his own token coinage in response to the shortage of small change brought about by wartime inflation. This, combined with the authorship of a series of radical pamphlets, led to his arrest and imprisonment in 1792, 1794, 1798 and 1801. The severity of his sufferings during a year in Shrewsbury gaol checked Spence's activism but his writings continued to attract disciples, most notably Arthur Thistlewood *(see p. 79).* Spenceans were later to be active in the Chartist movement *(see p. 85).*

William Godwin (1756-1836) having trained as a Dissenting minister at the renowned Hoxton Academy, renounced his faith to become an atheist and anarchist. Godwin's *Enquiry Concerning Political Justice and its Influence on General Virtue and Happiness* (1793) asserted that

"Truth is omnipotent … Man is perfectible or in other words susceptible of perpetual improvement." Taking it as axiomatic that men act according to reason Godwin concluded that it was impossible for a man to be rationally persuaded of a mode of behaviour and not to act accordingly. As reason taught benevolence it therefore inexorably followed that men, as inherently rational creatures, could live in harmony without laws or institutions. Any form of coercion must, therefore, be both corrupting and counter-productive. In 1794 Godwin published a pamphlet *Cursory Strictures,* supporting Tooke and his co-defendants, then arraigned on charges of treason. The same year also saw the publication of his ideological novel *Things as They Are; or, The Adventures of Caleb Williams.* In 1797 Godwin married the feminist Mary Wollstonecraft who had been deserted by the American father of her illegitimate child. Mary died the following year, giving birth to a daughter, also Mary, who grew up to marry Shelley and write *Frankenstein.*

James Gillray

James Gillray (1756-1815) was born in Chelsea, the son of a one-armed Chelsea Pensioner who had become the sexton of the Moravian burial-ground there. Initially apprenticed to a Holborn stationer to learn the arts of penmanship and engraving, Gillray was publishing satirical prints before he was out of his teens. In 1778 he was admitted to the Royal Academy Schools to study engraving under the Italian master Bartolozzi. Gillray's own output by then included portrait miniatures, book illustrations for works by Fielding and Goldsmith and reproductions of paintings.

A constitutional inability to suppress his idiosyncratic genius led Gillray to abandon the path of conventional artistic expression and from the age of thirty he concentrated on caricature. Rejecting the style of satire which relied on the viewer possessing an insider's knowledge of political symbols and icons, Gillray developed a sort of visual mimicry, cruelly distorting the appearance and personal traits of

54. The Prince Regent - one of Gillray's favourite targets.

the leading political figures of the day. The heavily-jowelled, stubble-chinned Fox became 'Black Charlie', the high-falutin' philosophizing sophistications of Burke's rhetoric led to his depiction as a bespectacled Jesuit, Sheridan's fondness for the bottle reduced him to a red-nosed sot. Members of the royal family from the king down were taken as equally fair game, viciously depicted as hideous in appearance, coarse in manner and at the same time both greedy and miserly in lifestyle. The louche, idle, spendthrift Prince of Wales, a friend of Fox into the bargain, was singled out for repeated ridicule as an adulterous, drunken voluptuary.

In 1797 Pitt, a regular target, temporarily bought off Gillray with a pension. Gillray also formed a discreet alliance with future Prime Minister George Canning, then a rising young Tory star. They were united in their detestation of Jacobinism in particular and all things French in general, one of the few consistencies in

Gillray's career as a political commentator. Once the Terror got under way Gillray's assaults on France and the French were unrestrained. Fox, as a supposed fellow-traveller, was scarcely less assailed. The emergence of Napoleon supplied Gillray with the hate-figure who became his greatest creation, the manic dwarf 'Little Boney'. Patriotism simultaneously required Gillray to abandon his ridiculing of the royal family and re-brand George III as the father of his people.

In 1798 Gillray settled over the print-shop at 27 St. James's Street, where his works were first displayed and chiefly sold. The death of both Pitt and Fox in 1806 deprived Gillray of two of his most favoured targets. Nelson, almost his only hero, had died the previous year. The satires of Gillray's later years became less directly political and directed more and more at social and personal issues, particularly fashions and the supposedly fashionable. Although he lived the life of an artisan Gillray's standing in relation to his art was unrivalled. Ironically both the king and the Prince of Wales were collectors of his work. Equally ironic was the admiration of the French artist David, iconographer of the Bonapartist regime. Gillray also enjoyed an appreciative following in Germany. George Cruickshank, who would inherit something of Gillray's mantle in the following generation, was a devoted disciple. Reserved, hyper-sensitive and melancholic, Gillray almost certainly suffered from depression and drank sufficiently heavily for it to be noticed and remarked on in an age noted for alcoholic excess. In 1807 his eyesight began to fail and he experienced a general breakdown in his health. Gillray's last signed print appeared in 1809. Lapsing into insanity in 1810, he attempted suicide the following year and finally died at 72 St. James's Street in 1815.

John Bull Personified

A large branch of Boot's the chemist on High Street, Kensington now occupies the site which was once a seed farm run by **William Cobbett** (1763-1835), a man of many incarnations. Born the son of a farmer and innkeeper in Farnham,

Surrey, Cobbett came to London at the age of nineteen. In 1784 he enlisted in the army and served in Nova Scotia and New Brunswick, rising to the rank of sergeant-major. Finding his officers mostly idle and incompetent, Cobbett took on far more responsibility than his rank implied and thus became privy to the widespread peculation practised in his regiment. When, in 1791, he attempted to expose these abuses he was forced by the counter-threat of legal action to flee to France, from where he emigrated to the newly-independent United States. Working as a bookseller and occasional writer in Philadelphia from 1792 to 1799 Cobbett, with typical contrariness, became a pugnacious defender of the mother country which he had been forced to flee, adopting the appropriately prickly pseudonym of 'Peter Porcupine' and penning enough criticism of America to fill twelve volumes. When Cobbett returned home in 1800 he did so with the reputation of a Tory patriot but scorned Pitt's offer to buy the services of his pen.

In 1802 Cobbett began publishing a *Weekly Political Register* which became the most influential radical newspaper of its day, ceasing publication only with his death. By 1806 he had become convinced of the need for major parliamentary reform. In 1810 his campaign in support of militiamen who had been flogged for trying to resist a pay-cut earned him a conviction for seditious libel, a fine of £1,000 and two years in Newgate prison.

In 1816 Cobbett drastically lowered the price of the *Political Register* to become what he himself dubbed his 'Twopenny Trash'. Cobbett's paper now reached the height of its popularity with a print-run of perhaps 50,000. As it was written to be read aloud in inns and workplaces it may have achieved a 'readership' of perhaps ten times as many. The suspension of *habeas corpus* in 1817 forced Cobbett to flee to America once again. Returning in 1819, he became a strident supporter of Queen Caroline *(see p. 79)*. In 1821 Cobbett undertook the lengthy peregrinations on horseback which were later written up to become his most memorable work, the *Rural Rides* (1830). Cobbett ended his career as MP for

55. '*William Cobbett quits his agricultural pursuits to become a soldier'. Coloured etching by Gillray in* The Life of William Cobbett, *by Cobbett, 1809.*

the new industrial constituency of Oldham (1833-35) in the first reformed Parliament. The nocturnal hours and indoor routine were profoundly unsuited to an habitual early riser and probably hastened his death.

Hazlitt noted perceptively of Cobbett that "as soon as anything is settled in his mind, he quarrels with it" but nevertheless hailed him as "a kind of fourth estate in the politics of the country" and was a warm admirer of Cobbett's "plain, broad, downright English". Carlyle with the detachment of a Scot styled him as "the pattern John Bull of his century". Cobbett appears at first sight to have been a Tory turned Radical but, while conducting a furious assault on the entire system of place-mongering, privilege and corruption which he called 'the Thing', he yet remained a traditionalist, appalled at the rise of the *rentier* culture and get-rich-quick mentality fostered by the war years which had bloated the government's bureaucracy and the National Debt. Cobbett yearned for what he recalled or imagined as a simpler, kinder, more honest England of stout yeoman farmers and proud artisans, a land in which the smoky factories and stinking slums which accompanied Britain's rapid industrialization were notable only by their absence. Cobbett especially championed the agricultural labourer of the south of England, immiserated by suppressed wage-levels and wartime taxes until he was reduced to living on a 'tea-kettle broth' of stale bread and onions. If Cobbett was consistent in anything it was in his hatred of the interlocking nexus of stock-jobbers, Jews and paper-money which was centred on and symbolized by the ever-expanding British capital which was London. Cobbett called it 'the Great Wen', a monstrous parasite on the body politic and hated it with a passion. Perhaps unsurprisingly the capital has never commemorated him with even a plaque, let alone a statue.

Noblesse Oblige

A patrician landowner, **Sir Francis Burdett** (1770-1844) was one of Horne Tooke's more unlikely acolytes. Burdett was in Paris during the early days of the French revolution and on his return in 1793 married into the Coutts banking dynasty. Financial independence made him free to indulge his radical convictions and spend freely on elections. A Member of Parliament at 26, he became a persistent thorn in the flesh of the authorities, attacking wartime taxation, the suspension of *habeas corpus* and the whole system of government by corruption and patronage. In 1807, after a protracted and turbulent campaign, Burdett became MP for Westminster, which he represented until 1837. In 1809 Burdett deliberately flouted the rule against reporting Parliamentary proceedings by allowing his speech in defence of a fellow radical to be published in Cobbett's *Political Register* and defied arrest in a four day siege. When he was committed to the Tower twenty-five thousand

troops were deployed onto the streets of London to control his enraged supporters in the biggest popular confrontation since the Gordon riots *(see p. 57)*.

The Observer's report of the triumphant procession which saluted Burdett's re-election in 1818 vividly illustrates the adulation he came to receive:

"The streets ... were thronged to excess; the windows and every nook and corner that afforded a view, being equally crowded. At two o'clock Sir Francis ascended the Car prepared for him at Hyde Park Corner Turnpike ... On the three steps at the foot of the chair were inscribed in gold letters "Reform" – "Truth" – "Justice" and the Car itself was richly covered with velvet ... Its great elevation gave the immense crowds assembled who lined the streets, an opportunity of seeing their Representative, who, by repeated bows, acknowledged their cheers. In a few moments after he took his seat, four rockets were discharged, in succession ... The procession then moved forward through Piccadilly ... They arrived in Covent Garden at ten minutes before five o'clock and from thence proceeded to the Crown and Anchor to dinner."

Burdett's criticism of the government's handling of the massacre of civilian demonstrators at 'Peterloo' outside Manchester earned him a fine of £2,000 and three months in gaol but thereafter his profile and influence began to wane. He devoted the last active phase of his parliamentary career to the cause of Catholic Emancipation, which was achieved as a result of the motion he himself had proposed. After 1837 he represented a Wiltshire constituency and in his declining years allied himself with the Conservatives.

CHAPTER SIX

Reaction and Reform

Fear of invasion and the effort to fight and finance a global war dominated the quarter century leading up to the defeat of Napoleon in 1815.

The early phases of the outbreak of revolution in France received a cautiously optimistic welcome in Britain as heralding a long overdue movement towards the sort of constitutional monarchy Britons had long enjoyed. A contrary view was, however, soon powerfully proclaimed in Edmund Burke's *Reflections on the Revolution in France* (1790) which presciently predicted that, after passing through increasing extremes of violence, the revolutionary movement would culminate in the dictatorship of an ambitious general. Writing from Paris Tom Paine *(see p. 67)* riposted with *The Rights of Man* (1791-2) which proved sufficiently popular in Britain to alarm the government of William Pitt. Unease among the ruling elite was reinforced by the establishment of proto-revolutionary bodies like the London Corresponding Society (1792), which sought to link up with similar groups of activists in the provinces. The execution of Louis XVI caused widespread revulsion in Britain, which was confirmed by first-hand accounts of 'the Terror' brought by an influx of thousands of dispossessed aristocrats and royalist sympathisers seeking safety across the Channel.

The government responded by passing an Aliens Act to enforce the registration of incomers and by recruiting a network of spies and informers. Faced with the possibility of ideological contamination the regime acted repressively and its repression largely worked as activist groups of tradesmen and artisans found themselves the objects of Home Office attention. In 1791 the Clerkenwell Close branch of the Constitutional Society was suppressed and in 1792 Bow Street Runners arrested members of the London Corresponding Society which habitually met at the Bull's Head in Jerusalem Passage in Clerkenwell. Nevertheless when the government called for a strengthening of national defences by the establishment of numerous Volunteer rifle companies radical Clerkenwell responded in May 1797 by establishing The Clerkenwell Association, recruiting "respectable tradesmen and honest workmen" whose character could be verified by local householders. Volunteers were required to drill for six hours a week and take part in occasional field exercises. In 1800 there was a massive general review of London Volunteer units in Hyde Park, where everyone got totally drenched. In that same year the Clerkenwell contingent came as close as they were ever destined to come to military action when detachments were assigned to the new local 'House of Correction', where inmates had rioted against its regime of forced labour and a starvation diet.

The atmosphere of public anxiety which accompanied the outbreak of war against the revolutionary regime in France was sustained by a succession of episodes which generated further periodic outbursts of alarm. In 1795 a 'Peace and Bread' rally was staged at Copenhagen Fields near the Caledonian Road *(see front jacket illustration)*. More surreptitiously would-be revolutionists, organised variously as United Irishmen and United Britons, plotted to co-ordinate a rising for Irish independence to coincide with a French invasion which would lead to a general revolutionary uprising in Britain itself. In November 1802 Colonel Edward

Despard (1751-1803), a former war-hero with a career grievance, who had been involved with both the United Irishmen and United Britons, was arrested. It was alleged that, from his headquarters near Soho Square, Despard was planning to use a cell of dedicated London Jacobins, supported by Irish malcontents, to mount a *coup d'etat* by seizing the Tower, the Bank of England and Woolwich Arsenal. Despite testimony to his good character from Nelson himself, Despard was convicted of plotting treason and, with six co-conspirators executed before a crowd of 20,000 at Newington.

The abortive Irish uprising of 1798 and the very real fear of a French invasion in 1802-3 provoked the establishment of further new companies of Volunteers and the enlargement of existing ones. By the time of the general review of 1803 the Clerkenwell Association numbered 701 infantry and 46 cavalry, commanded by the eminent clockmaker Francis Magniac, with the rank of major. Its ranks also included a chaplain, a surgeon, an assistant-surgeon and no less than eleven each of captains, first lieutenants and second lieutenants. One of the newest units present on that occasion was the rifle company raised by Barber Beaumont (1774-1841), a talented artist and financier, whose 'Duke of Cumberland's Sharpshooters' attained a standard of musketry fully equal to that of trained regulars.

In 1812 Spencer Perceval (1762-1812) achieved the unique and unenviable distinction of becoming the only British Prime Minister to be assassinated. A lawyer by trade, Perceval had come to prominence in acting as a junior counsel for the crown in the trials of such radicals as Tom Paine and Horne Tooke *(see p. 66)*. Singular in his personal piety and noteworthy in his diligence, Perceval proved an able MP and within five years was appointed solicitor-general, then attorney-general and Chancellor of the Exchequer before attaining the premiership in 1809. In May 1812 Perceval was assassinated in the lobby of the House of Commons by John Bellingham (1770-1812) a deranged Russia merchant who blamed the government for his

56. *Spencer Perceval.*

business failure. At his trial Bellingham's plea of insanity was rejected. He in turn declined to show any remorse before his execution.

Wellington's defeat of Napoleon at Waterloo was marked with celebrations of appropriate lavishness. The leaders of the victorious nations were feted and decorated and flatteringly memorialized on canvas by the able brush of Sir Thomas Lawrence. Wellington's staunch ally, the aged Prussian Blucher, memorably summarized his impression of Britain's capital in the pithy ejaculation "Was fur pflunder!" ("What a place to loot!").

Distress and Discontent

Post-war euphoria soon faded. The discharge of some half a million soldiers and sailors onto the labour market, coupled with the sudden ending of government war spending, produced widespread unemployment. In 1816 a mass-meeting at Spa Fields, Clerkenwell was intended by its organisers to spark off a general uprising but turned into a riot in which shops were sacked,

The Demon Drink

William Fitzstephen, writing ca. 1173, mentioned only two major drawbacks to living in London, the frequency of fires and "the immoderate drinking of fools" – 'binge-drinking' *avant la lettre*.

Brewing has been one of London's most large-scale and capital-intensive businesses since the Middle Ages. The Worshipful Company of Brewers received its charter in 1437 and over subsequent centuries contributed dozens of candidates to the service of the City as Alderman and Lord Mayor. Regulation by official inspectors of the quality of ale sold to the public is one of the oldest forms of consumer protection, dating back to at least the reign of Richard II, when retailers were required by statute to identify their premises by hanging out a sign. The granting and denial of licences for the sale of alcohol by inns and taverns was for centuries one of the major functions undertaken by local magistrates.

Excessive consumption of alcohol by ordinary Londoners became an overtly political issue during the reign of George II, when steady improvements in the output of the domestic harvest combined with a stagnation in population growth drove down the price of grain. This both lowered the cost of making gin and, by cutting the price of the main staple, bread, left the poor with spare cash for drink. Contemporary social critics like the magistrate and novelist Henry Fielding blamed general drunkenness for a dramatic rise in crime. Hogarth *(see p. 60)* vividly depicted the social degradation associated with the pernicious 'alien' spirit. Repeated attempts at legislative remedy failed until the Gin Act of 1751 finally banned distillers from direct sales to the public and restricted the retailing of spirits to premises worth at least £10 per year.

By the late eighteenth century London brewing was increasingly dominated by six major breweries. Some peculiarity of the British social sensibility decreed that brewers remained untarnished by the taint of 'trade' associated with almost every other manufacturing activity.

As gentlemen they were welcomed to the ranks of the political elite. Edmund Halsey, Master of the Brewers' Company in 1715, served as M.P. for Southwark. His successor as proprietor of the Anchor Brewery, Dr. Johnson's friend, Henry Thrale, likewise represented Southwark in the House. In the last five years of his parliamentary career Samuel Whitbread (1758-1815), a hyperactive critic of the government, spoke more often than any other Member, though to little constructive purpose. Sir Thomas Fowell Buxton (1786-1845) joined the Spitalfields brewery of Truman, Hanbury and Co. and in 1816 raised £43,369 at a single meeting at the Mansion House for the relief of unemployed Spitalfields weavers. He also founded a savings bank and fish market for the people of the area before

57. William Hogarth's famous depiction of Gin Lane, a comment on the effects of cheap gin on the poor. The scene is the slum area of St Giles-in-the-Fields. In the background is St George's, Bloomsbury.

58. A procession of the London Temperance League through Lincoln's Inn Fields in 1853.

taking over leadership of the anti-slavery movement from Wilberforce *(see p. 121)*. Frederick Charrington (1850-1936) renounced the family brewing business to devote himself to the cause of temperance in the East End and served as an original member of the LCC and of Stepney Borough Council.

The 1825 budget almost halved the duty on spirits, doubling legal consumption virtually overnight. The following decade witnessed the establishment, first of all in London, of the 'gin palace', a new style of 'public house', less like a domestic interior with tables and chairs than a retail shop with a bar counter, large plate-glass windows and garish gas-lighting. Designed for vertical drinking and maximum distributional efficiency, the gin palace dispensed with such traditional accompaniments to drinking as pub games or food. In an attempt to promote a less lethal alternative the Beer Act of 1830 made it possible for anyone to open a beerhouse by purchasing a two guinea (from 1834 3 guinea) licence. In reaction to the opening of more than 30,000 new beerhouses a temperance movement emerged through a series of individual initiatives in Preston, Leeds and Manchester, receiving strong support from Baptists, Congregationalists, Wesleyans and the Salvation Army. This Dissenting constituency came to overlap with supporters of the emerging Liberal Party, driving the 'beerage' into alliance with the Conservative party. In London a number of aristocratic landlords, like the Grosvenors in Pimlico and the Russells in Bloomsbury, strictly limited the number of liquor outlets on their estates. Temperance became a distinctive sub-culture, spawning its own organisations, most notably the Band of Hope, which targeted the young, and its own publications and institutions, including coffee-houses, restaurants, hotels, building societies, insurance companies and even a hospital and a music hall.

The temperance movement was political in two senses. Narrowly in that it sought to organise and agitate for legislative limitation on the drink trade, broadly in its propagation of total abstinence as the route to respectability and working-class self-advancement. As a mass-movement temperance provided a valuable training-ground in organisation and public speaking for many future Labour leaders, including Keir Hardie, Philip Snowden and Arthur Henderson. The often catastrophic effect of heavy drinking on family life in terms of domestic violence and wasted expenditure attracted women to the temperance cause, many of whom progressed to the suffrage movement *(see p. 109)*.

Strategically the temperance movement was hampered by an internal division between those who were prepared to tolerate drinking in moderation, like some Quakers and some Methodists, and the hard core activists of the United Kingdom Alliance who would settle for nothing less that total abstention. One tactic they could agree on was to cut back the number of liquor outlets by pressing magistrates to deny licences when they came up for renewal or to grant new ones only in return for the surrender of two or more existing ones. This, in many cases, the breweries were happy to do, sacrificing small, inefficient outlets for the opportunity to replace them with large, luxurious establishments capable of dispensing even larger quantities of drink with greater efficiency while at the same time enticing in potential customers by providing extra facilities such as billiard tables and live entertainment.

Alcohol consumption per head did decline markedly over the course of the century 1830-1930 but the extent to which this can be attributed to the earnest and often strident propaganda of the temperance movement is uncertain. There was a decline in jobs involving heavy manual labour in which it was deemed necessary to "put the sweat back in". Men became less inclined to seek nightly solace in the pub from homes which were becoming less squalid and less over-crowded. If organised religion notoriously lost its grip on an increasing proportion of Londoners, compared with the provinces and the countryside, the cult of respectability strengthened its hold. While a number of leading, and popular, political figures, like George Lansbury *(see p. 170)* were well known to be total abstainers their example commanded grudging respect rather than imitation.

Excessive drinking resurfaced as a political issue in the opening years of the twenty-first century with widespread condemnation from an emerging alliance of medical, clerical and judicial opinion, which linked the phenomenon with the traditional evils identified by the temperance campaigners of the past – public disorder and domestic violence – and added new concerns such as obesity and the burden on a hard-pressed National Health Service. While the national policy of 'New Labour' favoured fewer restrictions in the hope of creating a Continental 'cafe culture' of self-moderation, local political leaders, like Dame Jane Roberts, Labour leader of Camden Council, found their constituents responsive to the idea of stricter regulation under local control to impose limitations on hours and 'no go' areas for public consumption.

most alarmingly a gunsmith's. The government responded by suspending *habeas corpus*. Alleged ringleader Arthur Thistlewood (1774-1820) was tried for treason but acquitted following the failure of the prosecution to produce adequate evidence and the revelation that its chief informant, one Castles, was an *agent-provocateur* and convicted brothel-keeper. Thistlewood, born illegitimate, had in the course of a colourful career, lost an inherited fortune, failed as a farmer, succeeded temporarily as an army officer and developed a late vocation to become Britain's first professional terrorist. Following his acquittal he remained under Home Office surveillance.

Popular discontent was further aggravated by the manifest indifference of the Prince Regent to the distress of the poor as he continued to lavish money on his houses, his mistresses and himself. In 1817, amidst "a great deal of hissing and hooting", his coach was stoned as it went down the Mall en route from the opening of Parliament.

In February 1820 a plot to murder the entire Cabinet was foiled. The conspirators, led by Thistlewood, had been dissuaded from the hope of a spontaneous general uprising by the failure of the Spa Fields episode. Instead they planned to take advantage of a (falsely) rumoured dinner-party for the entire Cabinet, to be hosted by the Lord President of the Council, Lord Harrowby, at his Grosvenor Square residence, where the guests would be protected by minimal security. One of the plotters, a butcher, thoughtfully equipped himself with a couple of sacks for carrying away the murdered ministers' heads. Having thus disposed of the government the conspirators then planned to seize the Bank of England and Mansion House while setting the capital ablaze as a distraction. Thanks to efficient surveillance they were apprehended in a loft over a stable in Cato Street, off the Edgware Road. In the ensuing scuffle Thistlewood, an expert swordsman, killed a Bow Street officer. Thistlewood and five others were hanged and then decapitated and buried in quicklime the same day. Five others were transported to

ARTHUR THISTLEWOOD.

Exterior View.

59. *The apprehension of the Cato Street conspirators in a stable loft.*

Australia, where two them became policemen.

The death of George III in 1820 brought the Regent to the throne as George IV and simultaneously to a new low point in unpopularity. In 1795, as Prince of Wales, he had given in to parental pressure to marry Princess Caroline of Brunswick (1768-1821) in return having his massive personal debts paid off. After the briefest of consummations Caroline had taken herself off on a Continental odyssey accompanied by a bizarre menagerie of hangers-on. In 1820 the prospect of occupying a throne, even beside a consort whose loathing she heartily returned, brought her back to London, having refused an offer of £50,000 a year to relinquish her title and stay in exile. Caroline's status as a woman wronged was severely compromised by her own cheerful promiscuity. Her appeal as an ideal of femininity was similarly tarnished by her renowned indifference to elementary personal hygiene. The society beauty Lady Bessborough, who saw Caroline at a ball in 1815 found her to be "a short, very fat, elderly woman with an extremely red face", wearing a white gown cut "disgustingly low". It is therefore a measure of the popular contempt for the new king that Caroline's cause attracted large, noisy demonstrations of sympathy and support from crowds of ordinary Londoners who thronged St James's Square where she had taken up temporary residence. The king attempted to dispose of her by having a Bill of Pains and Penalties introduced into the House of Lords to divorce her and strip her of the title of Queen. When one of Caroline's counsel pleaded that Christ himself had forgiven the woman taken in adultery it proved a rhetorical flourish too far, prompting the chirpy refrain :

> *"Most gracious Queen, we thee implore*
> *To go away and sin no more;*
> *Or, if the effort be too great,*
> *To go away at any rate."*

The Bill was, however, withdrawn. Caroline then overplayed her hand by trying to gatecrash the king's coronation. This had been foreseen and was forestalled by the recruitment of a band of renowned pugilists under the captaincy of 'Gentleman' Jackson, who humiliatingly denied her access. Caroline then resolved the impasse by dying at Hammersmith a fortnight later.

The Utilitarians

The Enlightenment preoccupation with the possibility of advancing human happiness through the perfection of human institutions found an enthusiastic devotee in the person of Jeremy Bentham (1748-1832). Born in Spitalfields, educated at Westminster School, a teenage graduate of Oxford and a qualified

60. *Jeremy Bentham.*

barrister before he was twenty, Bentham never actually practised law. In *A Fragment on Government* (1776) he established his reputation as a political philosopher by assailing the traditional English constitution as lauded by Sir William Blackstone, whose lectures he had attended as an undergraduate and whose exposition of the principles of the English legal tradition exerted a profound influence on America's 'Founding Fathers' as they hammered out its new constitution. Bentham dismissed with contempt both the concept of natural rights ("nonsense upon stilts") and the sanctity of precedent as a guide to action. Bentham's *Introduction to the Principles of Morals and Legislation* (1789) elaborated his fundamental axiom that the overwhelming objective of law and politics should be the promotion of "the greatest happiness of the greatest number", which he believed to be capable of demonstrable calculation through the exercise of his 'felicific calculus', which evaluated pleasure and its opposite, pain, in terms of their certainty, immediacy, intensity, duration, replicability etc. As Newton's theories gained European currency through the popularised French version composed by Voltaire, so Bentham's did via the work of the Swiss scholar Etienne Dumont, bringing the philosopher honours from countries as diverse as revolutionary France and Tsarist Russia and the admiration of figures as different as Simon Bolivar, John Quincy Adams and Mehemet Ali Pasha of Egypt. As a consequence Bentham received a constant stream of distinguished visitors and acolytes at his London home in Queen Anne's Gate.

In Britain itself Benthamite scepticism of unthinking adherence to tradition quickened the assault on the politics of privilege and place, prompting demands for the reform of Parliament, the Common Law and a broad spectrum of institutions and services, ranging from public health to the relief of poverty, all of which could be subjected to cost-benefit analysis in terms of the utility principle. As far as London in particular was concerned Bentham's varied legacy ranged from the design and regime of Millbank prison as an exemplar of 'rational' penology to the establishment of *The Westminster Review* as an outlet for critical thinking and the foundation of University College, London as an instrument for its diffusion.

Bentham's most ardent disciple was Scottish-born James Mill (1773-1836). A disillusioned ex-preacher and hack journalist, Mill was re-energised by his discovery of Bentham's *oeuvre*, although he rejected its hedonistic implications in favour of a Calvinistic austerity and developed a psychological rationale for the Benthamite perspective. In a thousand essays and five books, most notably his *Essay on Government* (1820) Mill argued for the reform of law, pedagogy and politics – while at the same time rising to become head of the London-based bureaucracy of that state-within-the-state, the East India Company.

Mill's son, John Stuart Mill (1806-73) intensively educated by his father from the age of three, eventually succeeded to his father's bureaucratic eminence while far surpassing his intellectual influence through such works as *On Liberty* (1859), *Representative Government* (1861) and *The Subjection of Women* (1869). Subtler than Bentham, Mill understood how making the principle of communal welfare an overriding good could lead to the abuse of minorities and the oppression of individuals. As a Radical MP (1865-8) Mill exerted an important influence on the passage of the Second Reform Bill of 1867. Mill was honoured with a statue in the gardens outside Temple Underground Station. Sculpted by Thomas Woolner, it was unveiled just five years after his death.

Clubland

The Carlton Club was founded in the aftermath of the general election of 1832 in which the Tories were reduced to a rump of 179. The club took its name from its first, temporary premises at No. 2 Carlton House Terrace. By 1836 it was settled into premises in Pall Mall but, to accommodate an increased membership, these were rebuilt in 1854 to designs by Sydney Smirke and Disraeli's cousin, George Basevi. The moving spirits in the foundation of the Carlton were the party's principal agent F.R. Bonham (1785-1863) and Alexander Perceval (1787-1858), serjeant-at-arms of the House of Lords. Disraeli was elected a member in 1836. Gladstone, originally a firm Tory, was also an early member. In 1852 Gladstone was assailed by drunken members who threatened to throw him out of the window but did not resign until 1860. Disraeli had little fondness for club life but found it politic to look in periodically, most notably to bask in adulation after his supple manoeuvrings led to the successful passage of the 1867 Reform Act. The intellectual A.J. Balfour shared Disraeli's distaste, putting the Carlton into the same category as those other disagreeable accompaniments of a political career – long hours and constituents. In 1883 the Carlton Club became the venue for the launching of the Primrose League, a new mass-membership Conservative organisation intended to reach out to formerly excluded sections of the population such as women and Roman Catholics. On 19th October 1922 the Carlton provided the setting for a turning-point in British political history, when a meeting of backbench Tory MPs voted to withdraw Conservative support from the coalition government which had been headed by Liberal leader David Lloyd George since 1922.

Speakers' Corner

Hyde Park was used as an assembly point by Chartists on occasion but never became a regular place for their meetings or demonstrations. In 1855 a crowd of perhaps 150,000 people gathered at the park to demonstrate against Lord Robert Grosvenor's Sunday Trading Bill which, in the interests of strict Sabbath observance, proposed severe restrictions on the opening of shops, stalls and markets. If passed, this would have been a major inconvenience to the mass of working Londoners for whom Sunday was the only day free from labour. In 1866 and 1867 the Reform League organised mass demonstrations at Hyde Park to demand a further extension of the franchise, which led to clashes with police and the destruction of the railings along Park Lane. A right of assembly and free speech at the north-eastern corner of Hyde Park was subsequently recognised by the Royal Parks and Gardens Act of 1872. Speakers' Corner became an especially favoured venue for members of the early socialist movement who were excluded from other London locations by specially-framed park by-laws and restrictive interpretations of various Highways Acts. There are other Speakers' Corners in Finsbury Park, Kennington Park, Victoria Park and on Clapham Common and also in Sydney, Australia, Regina, Canada and Port of Spain, Trinidad.

Muddlesex

The imposing neo-Classical architecture of Regency London was expressive of order, harmony and rationality – and therefore somewhat at variance at how the metropolis was governed. The City was administered with tolerable efficiency by its ancient Corporation. The Corporation had, however, no interest in taking on wider responsibilities for areas beyond its boundaries – i.e. where, by 1811, 90% of a population of more than one million lived. The rest of London was subject to a morass of jurisdictions comprising seventy-eight parish vestries, the magistracies of Middlesex, Kent and Surrey, the Metropolitan Commissioners of Sewers and, authorised by some two hundred and fifty private Acts of Parliament, over three hundred local bodies – variously constituted as commissions, charities or trusts – with

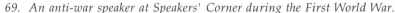

69. An anti-war speaker at Speakers' Corner during the First World War.

responsibilities for paving, policing, lighting, sewerage, poor relief or estate management and development – not to mention localities like the Inns of Court which were administratively autonomous. The districts for which a vestry might be responsible varied in size from the Liberty of the Old Artillery Ground, off Bishopsgate, which had a population of 1,500 at the time of the first census in 1801, to that of the wealthy parish of St. George's, Hanover Square, with a population of 60,000. Many jurisdictions competed or overlapped. Responsibility for paving the Strand, for example, could be plausibly attributed to no less than nine different bodies.

The work of cleansing, paving and lighting of the compact parish of St. Pancras was divided up between no less than twenty-one different bodies administering powers enshrined in thirty-five different Acts of Parliament. As the doyen of scholars of public administration, Prof. William Robson, was to note a century later there were "no regulations for their guidance, no attempt at uniformity of administration ... no security for the proper performance of their functions."

In the absence of any overarching authority, therefore, such major metropolitan improvements as the formation of Regent Street and the laying out of Trafalgar Square were executed, not by any municipal body, but by the Crown under the somewhat antiquated auspices of the Commissioners of Woods and Forests.

In 1831 John Cam Hobhouse, radical MP for Westminster attacked 'select' (i.e. oligarchic, co-optative) vestries for their exclusiveness and extravagances and succeeded in promoting an Act which required select vestries to become 'open' – i.e. elective – vestries wherever a majority of ratepayers wished for such a change. The ratepayers of St. Pancras. St. Marylebone, St. George's, Hanover Square, St. John's Westminster and St. James's, Westminster did so wish.

For fear of a confrontation with the Corporation of the City of London, the government of Lord Melbourne, engulfed in a flood of reforming legislation, declined to include London within the provisions of the Municipal Corporations Act of 1835, which brought a significant measure of democratic accountability to urban administration elsewhere throughout England and Wale. The 1835 Act embraced 178 towns and cities – but London, it was accepted, was different, different in scale, different in complexity and just – different. In 1837 a report of the Royal Commission on Municipal Corporations recommended a single elected government for the whole of London but Melbourne still opted for inaction.

In 1829 Sir Robert Peel effected the creation of a Metropolitan Police Force. Given Londoners' long-standing antipathy towards anything resembling a Parisian-style gendarmerie it was decided that constables should wear a blue uniform rather than the red traditionally worn by the military. That said, a very high proportion of the earliest intake was recruited from the ranks of ex-soldiers, over four-fifths of whom were discharged in the first five years for absenteeism, dishonesty or drunkenness. Hostility to the new institution was overcome only slowly. In 1831, when the first constable was killed on duty, while policing a rowdy Clerkenwell demonstration, the jury brought in a verdict of 'justifiable homicide'. As ever, the City Corporation was exempted from the provisions of the Act establishing the Metropolitan force and founded its own separate establishment in 1839.

In 1848 a Board of Sewers replaced eight separate commissions for sewers and assumed responsibility for flood protection. In 1854 a Royal Commission on the London Corporation rejected the idea of single municipal authority for the whole of London because, considered as a collectivity, a population of over two millions lacked the "minute local knowledge and community of interests" required for effective municipal administration.

A further degree of rationalisation was finally achieved in 1855. The parish vestries were reconstituted as elected bodies, the twenty-three largest remaining as distinct authorities, the other fifty-five being united into fifteen district

70. An early London police force. The policeman on the far right is wearing the new helmet, which replaced the impractical tall hats of his colleagues.

boards. By the same Metropolis Management Act a Metropolitan Board of Works was established to tackle major infrastructure projects over an area of 117 square miles, from Putney to Plumstead, from Hampstead to Lewisham. The Board's greatest achievement was the construction of the most extensive and advanced sewerage system in the world under the direction of its visionary chief engineer, Sir Joseph Bazalgette (1819-91). This banished for ever the menace of water-borne epidemics, most notably cholera. Bazalgette's project also involved the building of the Victoria, Albert and Chelsea Embankments. He subsequently built new Thames bridges at Putney, Hammersmith and Battersea. Other major MBW projects included forty road building or improvement schemes, including Queen Victoria Street, Shaftesbury Avenue, Charing Cross Road, Northumberland Avenue, Clerkenwell Road, Great Eastern Street, Burdett Road and Southwark Street. The Board also freed nine Thames Bridges from tolls, established the Metropolitan Fire Brigade,

bought Finsbury Park and Southwark Park, took control of Blackheath, Hackney Downs, Hampstead Heath, Parliament Hill and the Commons at Clapham and Tooting Bec and renamed three thousand streets. It also acquired responsibility for the enforcement of laws relating to the regulation of dairies and slaughterhouses, the suppression of 'baby farming', the demolition of insanitary housing, the storage of petroleum and explosives, the regulation of gas and water supplies and the safety of theatres and music halls – none of which saved it from extinction amid accusations of corruption on the 'Board of Perks'. Lacking historic roots or direct democratic endorsement or ancient and colourful ceremonies to celebrate its achievements or even its existence the MBW passed unmourned.

Let there be Light !

Gas-lighting made its London debut in 1807 as a political stunt when Pall Mall was illuminated to mark the birthday of the Prince of Wales. In 1812 the Gas-Light and Coke Co. received a

71. *An early manufacturing plant in the Horseferry Road of the Chartered Gas Company.*

charter of incorporation authorising it to provide light to the City, Westminster and Southwark. Gas was hailed not just as an amusing novelty but because, by literally throwing light on dark corners, it was considered an invaluable adjunct to the fight against street crime. The adoption of gas-lighting at Buckingham Palace and by the new Houses of Parliament in the 1840s gave the new technology the Establishment's stamp of approval. Eventually some twenty gas supply companies would be formed, some on a statutory basis, some not and none confined to clearly delimited areas of operation. Competition produced chaos until the companies themselves got together in 1857 to cartelise their operations on either side of the river, raise their prices and up their dividends. In 1860 they successfully procured an Act of Parliament endorsing their carve-up of the metropolis. The City was powerful enough in 1868 to get its own Act of exemption and to take over control of its own gas supply. The Metropolitan Board of Works attempted to emulate the City's success but failed although the 1875 Metropolitan Gas Companies Bill did at last manage to enforce standardisation in the quality of gas supplied. The advent of electricity in the 1880s encouraged the gas companies to promote their product for new uses, especially cooking, heating and lighting in working-class homes, a hitherto neglected market.

Two companies achieved dominance by relocating their operations eastwards to sites permitting much larger-scale operations, the Gas-Light and Coke Co. to Beckton, near East Ham and the South Metropolitan to the Greenwich peninsula. Following nationalisation by the 1945 Labour government the two companies metamorphosed into regional gas boards known respectively as North Thames Gas and South Eastern Gas.

One of a Kind

Born in Hoxton and educated locally, Charles Bradlaugh (1833-91) was briefly a teacher before leaving home as a teenager when preparation for confirmation provoked him to reject conventional religion. Radicalized by service with the army in Ireland, Bradlaugh found work as a solicitor's clerk and developed a parallel career as a lecturer, journalist and activist as editor and from 1862 owner of the *National Reformer*, President of the National Secular

72. *Charles Bradlaugh.*

Society and founder of the National Republican League. Bradlaugh supported the extension of the franchise and collaborated with Annie Besant *(see p. 105)* to propagate knowledge of birth control. In 1880 Bradlaugh was elected Member of Parliament for Northampton but declined to swear a Bible oath to perform his duties conscientiously, demanding instead the right, as an atheist, to make an affirmation. When this was refused Bradlaugh was re-elected by the voters of Northampton in 1881, 1882, 1884 and 1885. Bradlaugh was finally allowed to make an affirmation in 1886 and two years later succeeded in having that right enshrined in statute law. As a Member of Parliament Bradlaugh proved conscientious rather than controversial, though he did campaign forcefully for native rights in India.

And Another ...

The self-educated son of a Cornish carpenter, John Passmore Edwards (1823-1911) served his apprenticeship as an activist in the ranks of the Anti Corn Law League and the temperance movement *(see p. 76)*. Arriving in London in 1845, he became a prominent member of the Early Closing Association and the London Peace Society. Having started up an over-ambitious series of publications devoted to peace, politics and poetry, Edwards became bankrupt at thirty. Over the succeeding twenty years he paid off his debts in full and became the successful proprietor of the *Building News* and the *Mechanics' Magazine*. In 1876 he bought the first halfpenny newspaper, the *Echo*, from the notorious swindler, Albert Grant, and, working as his own editor, turned it into another success and a platform for his own personal crusades – the abolition of capital punishment and flogging, the suppression of gambling and the opium trade and the independence of the Boer republic of Transvaal.

73. *John Passmore Edwards.*

From 1880 to 1885 Edwards served as Liberal MP for Salisbury but became so disillusioned with the House of Commons that he renounced his parliamentary career to devote his later life to a careful campaign of philanthropy, chiefly to the benefit of his native county and his adopted city. Passmore Edwards founded five hospitals in London and fifteen libraries, as well as contributing to the art galleries at Whitechapel and Camberwell and the London School of Economics *(see p. 117)* and presenting a museum to West Ham and a public garden to Woolwich. He declined knighthoods from both Victoria and Edward VII but accepted the honorary freedom of the boroughs of East Ham and West Ham.

Victoria's London

Reigning for sixty-three years, longer than any other sovereign in British history, Queen Victoria attained an iconic status, although with scarcely any effort on her part. In terms of name alone her imprint on today's London remains ubiquitous. Victoria Street, driven through some of Westminster's worst slums in the 1840s, gave her name both to the station and to the area surrounding it. Queen Victoria Street was laid out in the City in the 1860s to link Bank Junction to a rebuilt Blackfriars Bridge, where the Queen's statue now stands. Victoria is also memorialised in the East End's Victoria Park, in the Victoria Dock, the Victoria Embankment, Victoria Square, in Queen's Gate, in the artisan suburb of Queen's Park and Queen's Woods at Highgate. Queensway was once Black Lion Lane where Victoria, growing up in Kensington Palace as the little Princess 'Drina', would take her daily carriage drive. On her accession the name was changed to Queen's Road, later to Queensway. In London's suburbs there are forty-two Victoria Roads, twelve Victoria Avenues, four Victoria Closes, three each of Victoria Crescents, Gardens and Groves and two Victoria Ways and Terraces. Almost a lifetime after the Queen's eventual demise the first post-war Underground line, opened in stages between 1968-71, was named the Victoria Line. Innumerable public houses likewise commemorate her name, not least the 'Queen Vic' in *Eastenders*.

Victoria's first act as monarch was to demand a bedroom separate from her overbearing mother, the Duchess of Kent. She then left Kensington Palace, where she had been born and grew up, to take up residence in Buckingham Palace, despite its unfinished state after more than a decade of supposed refurbishment, extension and upgrading. As a teen queen Victoria was addicted to dancing and the theatre. Marriage to the cultured and conscientious Prince Albert of Saxe-Coburg-Gotha brought a new seriousness to the queen's performance of her public duties. Albert encouraged the queen to take an active interest in the welfare of her subjects and especially of the poorer ones. The 'model dwellings', now at Kennington, which he had designed for the Great Exhibition, are a small reminder of the Prince's social awareness. Coincidentally the advent of railways and of advances in printing techniques which made the production of illustrated magazines much cheaper than before combined to enable the royal couple to be seen, both in the flesh, and as images of an ideal domesticity, by more of their subjects.

The opening of Albert's visionary project for a festival of culture and commerce, the Great Exhibition of 1851, was, the Queen confided to her diary, the proudest day of her life. A decade later the fulcrum of her existence was snatched away from her with Albert's premature death at the age of forty-two. Refusing all public duties for the following seven years, Victoria secluded herself away from London, either at Windsor or at the royal residences designed by Albert at Osborne and Balmoral. During this period a vigorous republican movement emerged, provoking the thoughtful editor of *The Economist*, Walter Bagehot, to compose a subtle defence of monarchy and a demolition of the republican case in his classic account of *The English Constitution*. Taking as his metaphor the colourful procession of the state opening of Parliament, when the Queen rode in splendour to proclaim 'her' political programme from the throne, Bagehot argued that such theatricality served the essential purpose of binding the unlettered masses to obey their betters, while their betters – readers of *The Economist* – well understood that real power was exercised by the boring men in dark suits who were quite eclipsed by the dazzle and glamour of the peers, courtiers and military escort which gave the throne its aura of authority. Britain, Bagehot argued, was in reality already a republic but it was dressed up as a monarchy – and necessarily so.

Cajoled by the Prince of Wales and her Prime Ministers into resuming public duties from 1868 onwards, Victoria was fortuitously assisted in regaining her subjects' affections by the near-fatal illness of the Prince of Wales in 1871. For weeks Londoners anxiously awaited news of each medical bulletin as the life of the normally robust heir to the throne hung in the balance.

87. *Emmeline Pankhurst.*

88. *Sylvia Pankhurst.*

the only working-class woman to attain a prominent leadership position amongst the suffragettes:

"Nuns in a convent were not watched over and supervised more strictly than were the organisers and members of the militant movement … It was an unwritten rule that there must be no concerts, no theatres, no smoking; work and sleep to prepare us for more work was the … order of the day … … we did so much more with our money than the party politicians. Mere hard work would tell … If a chair would be suitable as a platform, why pay a few shillings for a trolley? If the weather was fine, why hire a hall? If the pavements were dry, why not chalk advertisements of the meeting instead of paying printers' bills. If a tram would take us, why hire a taxi?"

In 1904 Mrs. Pankhurst held a meeting outside Parliament to protest the talking-out of a bill to grant women the vote. In 1905 Christabel

Pankhurst and Annie Kenney were arrested for the first militant action, heckling in the Free Trade Hall, Manchester. In 1906, as a reformist Liberal government replaced the Conservatives at the general election, the WSPU. relocated from Manchester to 4 Clement's Inn, off the Strand, conveniently in the shadow of the Royal Courts of Justice in the Strand and within a few minutes' walk of Bow Street Magistrates Court, where so many members of the movement would find themselves arraigned for infractions of the law. In the same year ten WSPU members were arrested at the House of Commons for causing a disturbance. Suffragists deplored such antics on the grounds that they provided ideological ammunition to those opponents of female suffrage who argued that women were incapable of reasoned debate and further that it jeopardised the fruits of non-confrontational pressure, such as the 1907 Qualification of Women Act which gave females the right to become borough and county-councillors and mayors.

In 1907 a 'Women's Parliament' met at Caxton

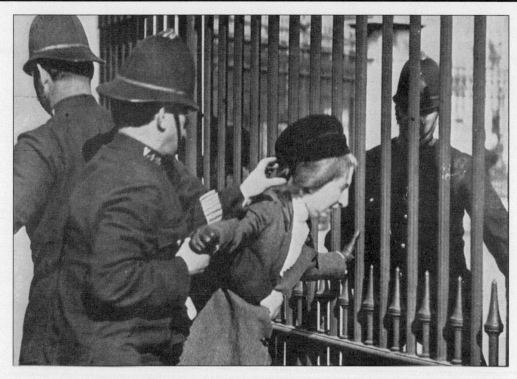

89. *A Suffragette arrested at the gates of Buckingham Palace.*

Hall, the WSPU began to publish its own newspaper *Votes for Women* and a Private Member's Bill to enfranchise women was defeated. In response to this disappointment the campaign of militancy was ratcheted up. In 1908 two suffragettes chained themselves to the railings of 10 Downing Street, a huge Women's Sunday demonstration was held as seven processions converged on Hyde Park, where supporters of the movement displayed seven hundred banners. In June the tactic of window-smashing to attract publicity was adopted. In 1909 a two week Women's Exhibition was held at Prince's Skating Rink in genteel Knightsbridge to raise funds for the movement, realising some £6,000. By then the WSPU was employing a paid staff of seventy-five. Fourteen suffragettes were sentenced to serve a month in Holloway for smashing the windows of government offices. When some of them went on hunger-strike in protest the authorities responded by forcible feeding. The failure in 1910 of a Conciliation Bill drafted to introduce woman suffrage provoked suffragette

riots outside Parliament in November, leading to 120 arrests and assaults by the police on many of the protesters. Many suffragettes refused to fill in census forms in 1911 as a means of registering their anger at being denied the full status of citizens. The coronation of George V provided another opportunity for a massive procession. The organisers claimed that sixty thousand women marched with a thousand banners and the support of a range of sympathetic organisations such as the Actresses' Franchise League, the Women Writers' Suffrage League and the Gymnastic Teachers' Suffrage Society. Suffragette action against property became increasingly violent, involving widespread window-smashing, leading to the arrest of some two hundred suffragettes. Militancy extended to the firing and bombing of churches, private houses and public amenities. Letters were ignited in pillar-boxes and buildings defaced with graffiti. WSPU headquarters at Clement's Inn was raided by the police in 1912. The WSPU responded by moving to larger premises at Lincoln's Inn House,

Kingsway. Christabel Pankhurst evaded arrest and went into self-exile in Paris, from where she could direct strategy safe from the possibility of arrest. In 1913 Emily Davison (1872-1913), a university graduate and devout Christian, was killed after trying to stop the King's horse during the Derby. The WSPU arranged a 'state funeral' for her at St. George's, Bloomsbury Way. In the same year the 'Cat and Mouse Act' was passed to frustrate hunger-striking. This allowed for hunger-strikers to be repeatedly released when their health was endangered and then summarily rearrested when they had recovered to serve out their sentences in stages. In 1914 Sylvia Pankhurst *(see p. 108)* was expelled from the WSPU. At the National Gallery Velazquez' Rokeby Venus was slashed in yet another publicity stunt. 'Slasher' Mary Richardson was sentenced to eighteen months with hard labour. Many art galleries were closed to the public or open only to men.

The militant tactics of the suffragettes hit the headlines, as they were intended to, but they were complemented by a sustained and ingenious strategy of marketing the movement and its ideology through an ever-growing range of publications, products, posters, banners and insignia. Much valuable input came from Sylvia Pankhurst, who had studied at the Royal College of Art. The suffragettes adopted an official colour scheme of purple, white and green, devised by Emmeline Pethick-Lawrence, co-editor of *Votes for Women* – "Purple as everyone knows is the royal colour. It stands for the royal blood that flows in the veins of every suffragette, the instinct of freedom and dignity ... white stands for purity in private and public life ... green is the colour of hope and the emblem of spring". These colours were represented on such various items as badges, buttons, handkerchiefs, rosettes, belts, slippers, sashes, scarves, hat-bands, ties, gowns, lingerie, necklaces, brooches, shoulder-bags, umbrellas, cushions, soaps and even tea-sets and bicycles. Christmas provided the opportunity for the sale of cards, crackers, calendars, stationery, albums, dolls, board games, playing cards, packeted tea and iced cakes from The Woman's Press shop at 156 Charing Cross Road, a location now occupied by Centrepoint, and from other WSPU shops in Bow, Chelsea, Chiswick, Fulham, Hackney, Hammersmith, Hampstead, Kensington, Kilburn, Lewisham, Limehouse, Mile End, Paddington, Poplar, Streatham, Sydenham, Wandsworth, Westminster and Wimbledon.

On the outbreak of war the Suffragettes suspended their agitation and demanded 'the right to serve'. Mrs. Pankhurst turned her formidable propaganda machine to recruiting men for the trenches and women for the factories. And not just the factories. Women drove lorries, operated cranes at the docks, worked on the buses and the Underground and cleaned out boilers at Beckton gas works. As the conflict drew to an end it was self-evident that the war could not have been won without the women. The 1918 Representation of the People Act gave women the vote at 30 if they were graduates, householders, wives of householders or occupiers of properties with an annual rental of at least £5. Eight million women thus became qualified to vote. Women were also given the right to become MPs. Mrs. Pankhurst stood for election as a candidate for the Women's Party, as the WSPU had been renamed, but failed to win a seat; in 1926 she was adopted as Conservative candidate for Whitechapel and St. George's. In 1919 the American-born Nancy, Lady Astor (née Langhorne), became the first woman to take her seat as a Member of Parliament. In the same year the Sex Disqualification Removal Act opened the civil service and professions to women. In 1928 the female voting age was reduced to 21, on a par with men and irrespective of property qualifications. Mrs. Pankhurst died three weeks after the passage of the enabling legislation. In 1929 Margaret Bondfield became the first female Cabinet Minister.

A statue honouring Mrs. Pankhurst was unveiled in the shadow of the Victoria Tower of the Houses of Parliament in 1930. Christabel went to America to preach the imminence of the Second Coming of Christ and was created DBE in 1936. Annie Kenney also gave up politics for religion, embraced theosophy and became an official of the Rosicrucian Order.

The Co-op

The origin of the modern co-operative movement is usually attributed to the formation in 1844 of the Rochdale Society of Equitable Pioneers. But their undoubtedly influential initiative was prefigured by much earlier enterprises, inspired by the philosophy of mutual assistance promoted by the industrialist and utopian visionary Robert Owen (1771-1858). In 1828 the future Chartist leader William Lovett was taken on as a storekeeper by the London Co-operative Trading Association. In 1832 Owen himself attempted to establish a Labour Bazaar in the Gray's Inn Road where goods would be manufactured and exchanged not for money but for 'labour notes' which represented the value of the labour that went into the goods made by participants. In practice the system quickly proved unworkable, as did most co-operative enterprises based on manufacture. Co-operative retailing on the Rochdale model, by contrast, became swiftly and strongly entrenched in the North of England, where it offered an alternative to 'tommy shops' run by exploitative employers. The co-op's 'cash only' policy avoided another common route to dependency, via extended credit. Given the relative absence of laws for consumer protection its scrupulous avoidance of adulterated goods proved another major virtue in the marketplace. Self-managed by elected committees and organised on a not-for-profit basis in which surplus funds were recycled to customers as an annual 'dividend', co-operative societies came to rank beside trade unions and independent chapels as schools of democratic experience. The formation of the Co-Operative Wholesale Society in 1863 enabled small, localised co-operative societies to collaborate as a single entity to take advantage of economies of scale in purchasing and to begin its own manufacturing operations and importing. This was soon followed by the establishment of an Insurance Society (1867) and a Bank (1872).

In the London region co-operative retailing began with the formation of the Royal Arsenal (1868) and Enfield (1872) societies, both of which could attract the purchasing-power of the high local concentration of well-paid craftsmen in the armaments factories of their respective localities. Others appeared in the hinterland of the large railway works at Stratford and in the burgeoning lower-middle class suburbs of south London, at Crays, Penge, Bromley and Croydon. As it proliferated 'Co-operativism' took on the character of a 'movement' with local societies organising self-improvement classes, libraries and even undertaking house-building. Dairy-farming, undertaking and travel agencies became major sectors of co-operative enterprise.

In 1883 a Women's Guild was formed in recognition of the degree of female participation in the activities of the movement. A Co-Operative Party was formally established in 1917. While maintaining a distinct identity for electoral purposes MPs elected as Co-operative candidates always took the Labour whip. In 1929 *Reynolds' News* was acquired to serve as the movement's journalistic arm.

In an increasingly competitive and sophisticated marketplace local co-operative societies were obliged to merge to survive. In 1918 the Bromley and Crays societies merged to become the South Suburban. In 1921 the Stratford, Edmonton and Brentwood societies came together as the London Co-operative Society. As late as 1945 nearly a quarter of British consumers were members of a co-operative society and some 20% of retail trade passed through co-operative branches. The movement proved, however, to be better at distribution than marketing and rapidly lost market share with the ending of wartime rationing. By the mid-1980s its share was down to 5%.

The success of the John Lewis Partnership in the second half of the twentieth century demonstrated that a model of co-operativism divorced from any linkage with Labour could offer a way forward while the most buoyant sector of the traditional movement proved to be its banking arm which attracted account-holders with its proclaimed policies of self-consciously ethical lending and investment.

90. *The headquarters of the Metropolitan Board of Works in Spring Gardens and the first, inadequate, home of the new London County Council.*

A Government for All London

The abolition of the Metropolitan Board of Works was followed by its replacement with the London County Council, which came into being in 1889 and took over the MBW's (inadequate) offices in Spring Gardens as well as inheriting its various responsibilities plus those traditionally exercised at Quarter Sessions, such as licensing places of entertainment. Although London had, by Act of Parliament, become a county, it was a county without history or traditions or the landowning gentry class from which shire counties conventionally recruited their governors. Indeed, so nugatory was the perception of its legitimacy that in devising titles the College of Arms was still ignoring the existence of a County of London over half a century after it came into existence, pointedly styling a new creation in 1944 as being 'of Chelsea in the County of Middlesex'.

Although the first chairman of the LCC, the Earl of Rosebery (1847-1929), had hoped that the council would be non-partisan, it was controlled by the self-styled Progressives (Liberals in all but name) until the rising rate bill and allegations of incompetence and waste led to their demise in an electoral landslide in 1907. From then until 1934 power was exercised by the Municipal Reformers (i.e. Conservatives). Meanwhile Labour replaced the Progressives as the second biggest grouping by 1925 and, once it had achieved power in 1934, retained it until the dissolution of the LCC in 1965.

The Progressives immediately inaugurated a programme of municipalisation to secure control of London's tramways and extended the Council's remit by promoting private Acts of Parliament. The Council used powers conferred by the 1890 Housing of the Working Classes Act to demolish the notorious slum area known as the Old Nichol and replace it with the architect-designed Boundary Street estate. The Public

Nor Any Drop to Drink?

By the sixteenth century water to supply Londoners came from as far away as Hackney and Hampstead. In 1581 the City Corporation approved a scheme by an alien entrepreneur, Peter Moritz, to inaugurate London's first pumped water-supply from London Bridge. From 1613 the New River Company, co-financed as a private speculation by royal jeweller Sir Hugh Myddelton and King James I, conveyed water from forty miles away in Hertfordshire to a reservoir in Clerkenwell for onward distribution.

The post-Fire expansion of London stimulated the formation of private water-supply companies at Shadwell (1669), York Buildings, off the Strand (1675), Hampstead (1692), Chelsea (1723), Southwark (1760) and Lambeth (1785). Five more companies were founded between 1805 and 1811. As commercial enterprises without legally demarcated boundaries these were often in direct rivalry, which led to much waste and nuisance through unco-ordinated pipelaying and maintenance. The Metropolitan Water Act of 1817 did at least require that henceforth all new water pipes should be of iron, which dramatically improved water pressure and reduced leakage.

There was greater concern in the nineteenth century for the quality as well as the availability of water supply. In 1827 Sir Francis Burdett *(see p. 73)* pilloried the Chelsea Water Company alleging that its water was polluted by "the contents of the great common sewers, the draining from dunghills and laystalls, the refuse of hospitals, slaughter-houses, colour, lead and soap works, drug mills and manufactories, and with all sorts of decomposed animal and vegetable substances". In response the Company constructed the first sand filtration system, which was eventually adopted by all other water suppliers.

Arthur Hassall's *Microscopic Examination of the Water supplied to the Inhabitants of London* indicted those water companies which still drew on the Thames as supplying water "in a high degree impure ... unfit for use and detrimental to health", exempting only the Chelsea Company "It is beyond dispute," he said, "that ... the inhabitants of the metropolis are made to consume ... a portion of their own excrement, and moreover, to pay for the privilege".

An Act of 1847 compelled the water companies, when requested, to maintain a constant flow, as well as requiring them to supply water for baths, wash-houses and street-cleansing. Nevertheless in 1850 London still had 80,000 houses, with 640,000 inhabitants, with no water supply. A further Act of 1852 finally made water companies move their intakes to the non-tidal reaches of the Thames above Teddington Lock and obliged them to filter all water intended for domestic use.

The researches of Dr. John Snow, prompted by the cholera outbreaks of 1848-49 and 1853-54, proved conclusively that the disease was water-borne but established opinion clung to the theory that it, and other epidemic infections, were the products of aerial 'miasma'. It was left to an environmental crisis – the 1858 sewerage accumulation known as 'the Great Stink' – to provide the impetus for action. When the nation's legislators found themselves choking on the stench from the Thames they at last hastily voted the £3,000,000 needed to implement the long-deferred scheme of the Metropolitan Board of Works chief engineer, Joseph Bazalgette, to construct the world's first modern sewer system.

As late as 1876 barely half of London's houses could rely on a constant supply of water. In the same year Captain Shaw reported on behalf of London's fire service that the water supply had proved inadequate at almost 600 incidents.

The sanitary reformer Edwin Chadwick had proposed buying out the water companies and putting supply in the hands of a public body as early as 1845. London's eight surviving private companies finally succumbed in 1902 with the passage of the Metropolis Water Act, establishing a Metropolitan Water Board, whose members represented the interests of the LCC, the Cities of London and Westminster, the Metropolitan Borough Councils and the local authorities of suburbs and counties within its five hundred square mile area of supply. The administration of the Metropolitan Water Board was subsequently transferred to a new Thames Water Authority in 1974 and this in turn was privatised as Thames Water in 1989.

91. Lord Rosebery.

established twenty-eight new metropolitan boroughs to function as a second tier of local administration. Most of the new boroughs were former vestries decked out with the novel civic paraphernalia of a mayor and aldermen. But others were formed by amalgamations. Stepney was created by a merger of Whitechapel, Mile End, Limehouse and St. George's in the East. St. George's, Hanover Square and St. Margaret's, Westminster joined St. James's, the Strand and St. Martin-in-the-Fields to become the City of Westminster. Wandsworth was merged with Battersea, Rotherhithe with Bermondsey, Woolwich with Plumstead and Holborn with St. Giles. The new metropolitan boroughs had significantly greater powers than the vestries and district boards they superseded, with responsibility for paving, lighting and sanitation and the provision of public facilities such as baths, washhouses, libraries and cemeteries. They were also empowered to buy land and build houses. There were marked disparities between boroughs in the extent to which they interpreted and developed what they took to be their proper functions. Fifteen of the boroughs became major suppliers of electricity to their localities. Camberwell played the cultural card, opening a fine art gallery as early as 1902 and providing six libraries. (Paddington waited until 1930 to open its *first* library.) Battersea had built a pub-free housing estate by 1903 and provided subsidized milk for infants. But only six boroughs even attempted programmes of slum clearance and even they had achieved only a niggardly seven acres between them by 1914.

Health (London) Act of 1891 led to the assumption of responsibility for nursing homes, midwife training, ambulances, institutions for the blind and mentally retarded and the treatment of venereal diseases and TB. The London Building Act of 1894 set more rigorous construction standards and took account of the new materials and technologies being adopted in the building industry. In the same year Hackney Marsh was acquired and saved from being built over. The opportunity to plug a large gap in the capital's education system led to the creation of eighteen polytechnics and technical institutes. In 1897 the Blackwall Tunnel, planned but not begun by the MBW, was opened to traffic.

Alarmed by the new London County Council's vigour in exercising its powers and eagerness to seek new ones, in 1899 the government, as a counterweight to the power of the LCC,

The LCC continued unabashed to press forward with major infrastructure projects and the extension of its functions. LCC officials inspected lodging houses, slaughterhouses, cowsheds, dangerous buildings, historic properties and weights and measures. They also registered midwives and administered the 'blue plaque' scheme. By 1903 London's tramways had been brought into a single municipally controlled system and converted to electric power. Horses were similarly phased out in the fire service. In 1903 Hainault Forest was acquired as a recreational area. In 1904 the LCC took over the duties of the London School Board, assuming responsibility for three-quarters of a million children, seventeen thousand teachers and nine hundred and forty schools. In 1906 a threat to build over Edwardes Square in Kensington led the Council to secure the passage of the London Squares and Enclosures Preservation Act to ward off such usurpations. Kingsway and its associated tram tunnel were built to ease traffic congestion between the Euston Road and the Embankment. A second tunnel under the river was opened at Rotherhithe in 1908 and pedestrian tunnels at Greenwich and Woolwich. New bridges were opened at Battersea and Vauxhall.

In 1909 work began on clearing a site to accommodate an appropriately palatial headquarters building for a municipal government which, if no longer Progressive was still self-consciously self-confident. That said, "the greatest municipal authority in the world" was still rather a muddle as its own Chief Clerk, the erudite antiquarian Sir Lawrence Gomme confessed:

92. *The London School of Economics, 2007.*

"The whole makes up a conglomerate which cannot be styled local government in any sense ... London, the capital of the empire, with a glorious history, is under the heels of many interests, many cliques and parties, which play one against the other and never play for the community."

Muddle or not, the LCC continued to expand its responsibilities and resources inexorably. In the early 1890s LCC employees represented 1 in 519 of London's workforce; by the 1920s the figure would be one in 38.

London School of Economics
The foundation in 1895 of the London School of Economics was made possible by the bequest of £20,000 by Fabian Henry Hunt Hutchinson and initiated by Sidney and Beatrice Webb, George Bernard Shaw and Graham Wallas (1858-1932). Modelled on *L'Ecole Libre des Sciences Politiques* in Paris, the London School of Economic and Political Science was incorporated in the form of a limited company, obviating the alternative of petitioning for a Royal Charter. Its purpose was defined as "the study and advancement of Economics or Political Economy, Political Science or Political Philosophy, Statistics, Sociology, History, Geography and any subject cognate to any of these." In 1899 the Director presciently noted that the infant institution was already drawing students from sixteen different countries. A century later the number of countries would be over a hundred and thirty. As Director Ralf Dahrendorf would note in his centenary history of the School, it was neither 'British' nor 'National', "its base was London and its home the world."

LSE would establish the first British chairs in sociology, economic history and social anthropology. Although many of its staff would make distinguished contributions to the methodologies of their disciplines, the School would also exert a profound effect on the formulation of practical policies. At the opening of the twenty-first century LSE would have Centres or Units devoted to studying Social Exclusion, Civil Society, Economic Performance, Environmental Policy, Global Governance, Human Rights and European Foreign Policy.

The School was first located at No. 9 John Street, Adelphi but soon moved to No. 10 Adelphi Terrace, later the home of George Bernard Shaw. The British Library of Political and Economic Science was established at No. 19 Adelphi Terrace in 1896. In 1900 the LSE was recognised as a constituent college of the federal University of London. In 1902 the School moved to Clare Market, a site provided by the London County Council. Money for a building was donated by Passmore Edwards. New buildings were opened in the 1920s, 1930s and 1960s and major new extensions in 1970 when the School also took over the former head office of W. H. Smith in Portugal Street.

The staff of the London School of Economics reads as a roll-call of intellectual distinction.

Sir Halford Mackinder (1861-1947), Director from 1903 to 1908, became a Member of Parliament (1910-22) and Privy Councillor. A pioneer of geography as a serious academic discipline, he developed the 'Heartland' theory of 'geopolitics' (a term he disliked), which is alleged to have greatly influenced Hitler's world view. A.V. Dicey (1835-1908) was the outstanding constitutional lawyer of his generation. Harold Laski, a future Chairman of the Labour Party. joined the faculty in 1920, when Attlee was also on the staff *(see p. 171)*. Attlee's Chancellor of the Exchequer, Hugh Dalton (1887-1962) was another LSE lecturer. Sir Arthur Bowley (1869-1957) pioneered the calculation of the National Income and directed the *New Survey of London Life and Labour* (1930-35). Sir Dudley Stamp (1898-1966) directed the Land Utilisation Survey of Britain. Economic historian R.H. Tawney (1880-1962) became President of the Workers' Educational Association. Philip Noel-Baker (1889-1982), captain of the British Olympic team in 1920 and

1924 and holder of one of the earliest chairs in International Relations was to be awarded the Nobel Peace Prize in 1959 for his lifelong efforts for disarmament. William, Lord Beveridge (1879-1963), Director of the School from 1919 to 1937, as author of the 1942 Beveridge Report on social services delineated the framework of Britain's post-war welfare State. Lionel, Lord Robbins (1898-1984), Professor of Economics from 1929 to 1961, directed the economic section of Churchill's War Cabinet and in the 1960s wrote the landmark report which led to an unprecedented expansion of higher education. In 1933 Robbins and Beveridge jointly led the LSE. initiative which led to the establishment of the Academic Assistance Council which helped over two thousand academics escape from fascist persecution in Europe and relocate to one of the democracies.

Contrary to popular perception LSE faculty have also included heavyweights of the political Right as well as the Left. Friedrich von Hayek (1899-1992), author of *The Road to Serfdom* (1944) and winner of the 1974 Nobel Prize for Economics was one of Margaret Thatcher's chosen mentors. Sir Karl Popper (1902-94) and Michael Oakeshott (1901-90) were similarly of the philosophical, if not actively political, Right. Director and sociologist Anthony Giddens, author of 'the Third Way', served as Tony Blair's intellectual guru. Prof. Amartya Sen (1933-) was awarded the Nobel Prize for Economics in 1998.

Graduates of the LSE have included Prime Ministers of Barbados, Dominica, St. Lucia, Jamaica (two), and Mauritius and two Presidents of Ghana, two of Kenya and one each of Fiji, Kiribati and India. The writers of *Yes, Minister* made their famous fictional hero, Jim Hacker, a graduate of LSE and the creator of *The West Wing* conferred a doctorate from LSE on 'President Bartlet'. In the words of *The London Encyclopaedia* "the School has probably had more influence on the political shape of the present-day world than any other university school."

Population Politics

The relentless expansion of London's population since the sixteenth century has periodically prompted political initiatives to achieve demographic displacement.

In 1619 the City fathers acceded to a request of the Virginia Company to despatch a hundred Bridewell children to their fever-ridden infant colony. All but a dozen or so died within a year. A century later the philanthropic general James Oglethorpe (1696-1785) conceived the novel experiment of peopling a new American colony, Georgia, with London's petty offenders and minor debtors, as an alternative to their incarceration. After the loss of the American colonies New South Wales and Tasmania were adopted as new dumping grounds for the criminal classes – including political dissidents – 164,000 of them by the time transportation was finally ended in 1868. The settlement of South Australia and New Zealand, funded largely by City rather than public funds, were on quite different lines, migrants being selected rather than sent and chosen for their skills rather than their misdemeanours, in accordance with the principles of systematic colonization first worked out by Edward Gibbon Wakefield (1796-1862) as he languished in a London prison in consequence of a botched elopement.

Subsidized emigration to the outposts of empire was seized on by numerous Victorian churches and charities as a means of relieving London of its teeming poor and especially of the rootless young who might otherwise turn to crime or radical politics. Vast, empty, labour-hungry Canada was a destination favoured alike by Dr. Barnardo, William Booth and Baroness Burdett-Coutts, who endowed two entire villages in British Columbia for the reception of emigrants. The Bethnal Green Medical Mission, which ran a large Sunday school from whose ranks "steady and industrious" candidates were chosen, was still sending children to Canada as late as 1925. The East End Emigration Club, one of several similarly-titled organizations targeted on London's poorest districts, was largely financed by the British and Colonial Emigration Fund, which was chaired by the Lord Mayor, and was supported by the Poplar Board of Guardians which chipped in modest per capita grants to clear potential dependents off its books.

In the later stages of the Chartist movement (see p. 85) several of its leaders became beguiled with the notion of establishing Utopian rural communities to which London's poor could be decanted, a notion hopelessly at odds with contemporary trends in an agricultural sector which was becoming increasingly mechanized and capital-intensive and, from the 1880s, in increasingly intensive competition with overseas producers. That said, William Booth did succeed in establishing a successful agricultural colony in Essex on the eve of the Great War but on too modest a scale to make any serious impact on London's *lumpenproletariat*.

Professor Patrick Abercrombie's wartime plan (see p. 163) for the redevelopment of the County of London envisaged dispersing some 600,000 persons from the central districts of the metropolis, including half the population of Bethnal Green, Stepney, Shoreditch and Southwark. The success of the dozen post-war 'New Towns' developed beyond the Green Belt at Harlow, Basildon, Crawley etc. represented a partial, if less draconian, realisation of this vision. Since then successive governments have intermittently attempted to decentralise sections of the public sector, despatching the Royal Mint to Wales and relocating the administration of social security in Newcastle Upon Tyne, though less perhaps in a serious effort to decongest London than with the intention of creating employment in de-industrialized localities. The suggestion that significant numbers of Treasury mandarins might be settled in, say, Manchester was greeted as a flight of political fantasy.

CHAPTER EIGHT

Emigrés, Exiles and Immigrants

Prologue to Diversity

London is now claimed to be the world's most multicultural city, home to some forty ethnic groups of ten thousand or more. More than three hundred languages are spoken in the metropolis. Ethnic minorities account for a quarter of the capital's population. A sixth of the resident population was born outside the U.K. London's cosmopolitanism is, moreover, by no means a recent phenomenon. A century ago an Edwardian guidebook boasted that London had "more Scotchmen than Edinburgh, more Irish than Dublin, more Jews than in Palestine and more Catholics than in Rome."

If most of the inhabitants of Roman *Londinium* were still local Britons with a thin veneer of 'Romanitas', they at least rubbed shoulders with officials, merchants, soldiers and slaves drawn from all quarters of the Roman empire. Anglo-Saxon London also accommodated enough Danes for them to constitute a distinct community around the Aldwych church of St. Clement to give it its by-name of St. Clement Danes. Jews from Rouen came with the Conqueror. Expelled en masse in 1290, they returned, led by a vanguard of wealthy Sephardim from Amsterdam, with Cromwell's hesitant approval in 1656. Flemish craftsmen were recruited by Edward III. Initially welcomed as weavers, they were later valued as brewers, builders and bawds. The rise of Protestantism created a new motive for migration. French Huguenots and Dutch Calvinists were welcomed by Edward VI *(see p. 31)*. The Revocation of the Edict of Nantes in 1685 led to a further influx of Huguenots, perhaps as many as forty thousand. Skilled and thrifty, they were of immense benefit to London's economy. The first Governor of the Bank of England was a Huguenot, Sir John Houblon, and so were six of his fellow directors. Another Huguenot, Ligonier, became Commander-in-Chief of the British Army. Over sixty Huguenots served as Members of Parliament over the course of the eighteenth century.

Am I Not a Man and a Brother?

London's black population, estimated at twenty thousand in the eighteenth century, was a by-product of the slave trade. Whether it constituted a community is problematic. Although there are instances of black people gathering together to sing and socialize they did not have the resources to maintain distinctive institutions. There were no black churches or black schools. Denied access to apprenticeships, most black people were employed in domestic service and thus isolated from one another. Their social standing as status symbols is evident from their routine inclusion in society portraiture, although down-market examples can also readily be seen in the engravings of Hogarth or the caricatures of Rowlandson. A few served in the army, mostly as musicians. A semi-criminal element of casual labourers, street-hustlers and entertainers clustered around St. Giles and in the riverside parishes of the East End.

A few black individuals did, however, become persons of consequence, most notably Ignatius Sancho (1729-80). Born on a slave ship, brought up as a servant in Greenwich, Sancho educated himself, became a butler and ended up owning a posh grocery store off Whitehall. Gainsborough painted his portrait. Sterne conducted a literary correspondence with him. He composed music and had it published. As the owner of a business he voted in Westminster elections. Sancho was

93. *William Wilberforce; oil by George Richmond.*

94. *Olaudah Equiano (see p. 122), purchased his freedom in 1766 and from 1786, when he lived in Marylebone, he was active in the campaign to end the African slave trade.*

the only black person of the century to have an obituary notice of his death in the press. Above all he was a living disproof of the notion that people of African descent were in any way inherently inferior to Europeans or incapable of living a civilised, indeed cultured, existence.

London was to play a pivotal role in the abolition of the slave trade from which it had so greatly benefited. The vicar of St. Mary Woolnoth, John Newton (1725-1807), himself a former captain of a slave ship, preached the sermons which set the anti-slavery movement alight and in his hymn *Amazing Grace* gave it an anthem. The landmark case of the runaway slave James Somersett, heard in London before Lord Justice Mansfield in 1772, determined that slavery had no legal standing on English soil and that runaways could not forcibly be returned to their former masters. Former black Loyalists, who had fought for Britain during America's war for independence and been repatriated to London, were recruited to form the first settlers of the initially ill-fated colony of Sierra Leone.

William Wilberforce (1759-1833) was MP for Hull but led the campaign for abolition from his London home. London brewers Samuel Whitbread (1764-1815) and Thomas Buxton (1786-1845) were influential allies of the cause. The West Indian 'plantocracy' arrayed against them a powerful caucus of opposing spokesmen in the City and in the House of Commons. The abolitionists responded by organising boycotts of sugar and rum and deluging Parliament with more petitions than it had ever received on any topic in its whole long history. The outbreak of war against revolutionary France temporarily retarded the momentum of the movement but even that could not long delay it and Parliament decreed the trade abolished throughout the British Empire in 1806. The rearguard action fought by a West Indian interest intent on extracting compensation for its loss of human property held back the abolition of slavery itself until 1833 and, in practice, until 1838.

A plaque marks the home in Marylebone of Olaudah Equiano (?1750-97) whose *Interesting Narrative* gave an autobiographical account of how he had himself been kidnapped, enslaved and maltreated. Wilberforce was commemorated shortly after his death with a statue in Westminster Abbey. The name of Thomas Clarkson (1760-1846), his indefatigable researcher, has belatedly received due recognition in the window above Poets' Corner. John Newton's pulpit and the eloquent epitaph he composed for himself can still be seen in St. Mary Woolnoth. An elaborate Gothic fountain in Victoria Tower Gardens salutes the efforts of Buxton who, succeeding Wilberforce as the parliamentary leader of the abolitionist movement in 1823, secured the end of slavery a decade later.

The French

A plaque placed by Westminster City Council records the lodgings at 10, Maiden Lane which were in 1727-28 the home of Voltaire (1694-1778). Conveniently close to the literary coffee-houses of Covent Garden, it was an ideal location from which to encounter Pope, Swift, Congreve and Berkeley, all of whom he met during his sojourn. Hailed as a dramatist and poet, Voltaire became a lifelong Anglophile thanks to a chance encounter with the exiled Tory leader Bolingbroke which set him to learning English so that he could read Locke *(see p. 50)* in the original. Causing offence to an aristocrat then led to a beating, a turn in the Bastille and a one-way trip to Calais to take the boat for Dover. Voltaire stayed in England for over two years, perfecting his command of both spoken and written English to the point of keeping his notes in English. London's vigorous intellectual life confirmed his admiration for a nation of merchant princes which had proved victorious over the armies and navy of the supposedly most mighty monarch in Europe, Louis XIV. Voltaire became convinced that personal liberty and freedom of

95. Voltaire.

discussion provided the context in which it had been possible for the thought of such giants as Locke and Newton to emerge. Comparing their work with the speculative rationalisations of Descartes and Pascal, he found his countrymen wanting. But the most important outcome of Voltaire's London years was the volume of *Lettres Philosophiques* (1734), a manifesto of modernism, in which he introduced to his compatriots the achievements of English liberty and English letters – Locke, Newton – and even Shakespeare.

The revolutionary 'Terror' unleashed in France in 1793 led to a mass-migration of aristocrats, royalists and over two thousand Catholic priests. This influx prompted a softening of traditional Protestant bigotry, leading to the establishment of new Catholic chapels and paving the way towards the eventual restoration of full civil liberties to Catholics in 1829.

The supple Charles Talleyrand (1754-1838) came to London three times in 1792-3 on behalf

96. 'Celebrities in Hyde Park', featuring, from the left, the Duke of Wellington, Mrs Arbuthnot, Talleyrand and Count D'Orsay. Note the Achilles monument to Wellington in the background.

of the revolutionary French government in an attempt to keep Britain neutral until he, too, found himself on the list of *persona non grata* and was forced to flee to the USA. Talleyrand's name is recorded on the shell-canopied door of No. 11 Kensington Square as a former resident. Having survived and served every regime for almost four decades, Talleyrand returned to London once more in 1830 as ambassador for the new Orleanist monarchy, residing at 21 Hanover Square until his retirement in 1834.

Germaine Necker (1766-1817), daughter of the last finance minister of the *ancien regime*, came to London in 1813 at the end of a twenty year exile during which she had established a formidable European reputation as a novelist, dramatist and political commentator, a reputation confirmed by the publication that year of an English translation of her *magnum opus*, an analysis of German culture and civilization in which she popularised the notion of 'Romanticism'. Known by then as the widowed Madame de Stael, she stayed until the following

year. A plaque marks the site of her temporary residence in Argyll Street, just off Oxford Circus. Mme de Stael's last work appeared posthumously a year after her death in both French and English editions. In her *Considerations on the Principal Events of the French Revolution* she held up the English political system as the model for post-revolutionary France.

Charles X (1757-1836), the last Bourbon monarch, who assumed the throne in 1824 and was overthrown by the Orleanists, had from 1811 to 1820, waited for his turn on the throne in modest surroundings at 72 South Audley Street. An even less useful acquisition was the Duke of Normandy who styled himself Louis XVII and was a familiar sight on Regent Street.

Some, at least, of the refugees from the revolution came with prodigious talents, rather than grievances – and came to stay.

Marc Brunel (1769-1849), a former royalist naval officer, made a major contribution to Britain's war-effort by designing an integrated set of machine-tools for mass-producing ship's

97. Sir Marc Brunel.

pulley-blocks in Portsmouth dockyard. He went on to build the first tunnel in the world to run under a river, between Wapping and Rotherhithe and to father, educate and train the greatest engineer of the century, Isambard Kingdom Brunel (1806-59). Brunel senior's achievements were recognised with a knighthood. A plaque marks his residence at 98 Cheyne Walk, Chelsea. Architect Augustus Charles Pugin (1762-1832) fathered and trained Augustus Welby Northmore Pugin (1812-52), pioneer of the Gothic Revival and designer of the décor of the Houses of Parliament *(see p. 84)*. A bronze plaque marks their home at 106 Great Russell Street, Bloomsbury.

The revolution of 1830, which overthrew the restored Bourbon monarchy, brought a new wave of émigrés as the French radical Flora Tristan observed when visiting London in 1839 – "after every Paris uprising … eddies have always been felt in the monster city." One of the most distinguished of the newcomers was the chef Alexis Soyer (1809-58). A 'celebrity chef' *avant la lettre*, Soyer had just been taken on in the household of Prince Polignac when the revolution deprived his employer of his position

at the Quai d'Orsee and Soyer of his job. In 1837 Soyer was appointed chef at the recently-established Reform Club *(see p. 83)*, then housed in temporary premises at 104 Pall Mall and subsequently removed to Gwydyr House on Whitehall. Notwithstanding these disruptions, on the occasion of Victoria's coronation in 1838, Soyer rose triumphantly to the challenge of serving breakfast to some two thousand people. When the Reform finally moved into its permanent Pall Mall premises in 1841 Soyer installed state-of-the-art gas-ovens which became the talk of culinary London and one of the more unusual of the city's tourist attractions. Throughout his dazzling career as a caterer Soyer also displayed a creditable civic consciousness organizing emergency soup kitchens during the great Irish famine, publishing a book of recipes for the poor and, during the Crimean War, reorganising the diets and victualling system at Florence Nightingale's hospitals *(see p. 86)*.

Louis-Napoleon Bonaparte (1808-73), nephew of the late Napoleon, after the failure of an attempted coup at Strasbourg settled in London in 1838. Another failed coup at Boulogne in 1840 led to an imprisonment, from which he escaped, fleeing again to London in May 1846. On the outbreak of revolution in France in February 1848 he became president of the new republic before seizing personal power in a coup to reinstate an imperial regime. One of the most lasting of his regime's achievements was the dramatic reconstruction of central Paris under the direction of Baron Haussmann, a sometimes brutal programme of modernisation inspired at least in part by admiration for the London in which his imperial master had lived as an ambitious exile. When Napoleon III's empire collapsed as a result of defeat in the Franco-Prussian war of 1870-71 he returned to London, settling and dying at Chislehurst. The plaque marking his former residence at 1c King Street, St. James's was already in place, having been erected in 1867.

The events of 1870-71, most notably the bloody suppression of the revolutionary Paris

Commune, brought another wave of French émigrés to London, where they founded a Communist club which met in Rupert Street.

The Liberators

Napoleon's invasion of Spain in 1808 gave Spanish colonies in Latin America the chance to seize their independence from metropolitan rule. British trading interests favoured this development for opening up potentially profitable markets from which they had previously been excluded. London became the most promising place for revolutionary regimes to begin their search for international diplomatic recognition, to raise financial loans and, as the wars against France ended, to recruit experienced officers and veterans for their armies and navies.

The groundwork for independence had been laid by alienated intellectuals like the Peruvian Jesuit Juan Pablo Viscardo Y Guzman (1748-98) whose *Letter to the Spanish Americans*, denouncing Spanish rule as tyranny and calling for Latin American independence, was composed in London in 1791. Guzman died in poverty in Soho, where he is commemorated by a memorial in St. Patrick's church. His *Letter* was first published in 1799, in London, in French, and then in Spanish in 1801.

The ultimate fate of Francisco de Miranda (1750-1816) was to be even more tragic than that of Guzman, although Miranda at least was subsequently recognised as 'El Precursor', the forerunner. Born in Caracas, at 22 he went to Cuba to fight against the British in one of the subsidiary campaigns of the American War for Independence. Accused of misuse of funds, in 1783 Miranda, protesting his innocence, fled to the infant United States, where he met the leaders of the American revolution and became inspired by the idea of liberating Spanish America. Harassed by Spanish agents, Miranda fled to London, where he was able to present his cause to Prime Minister William Pitt in 1790. Pitt extended him protection and encouragement but gave no concrete assistance. Miranda next tried his luck in revolutionary France, where he served the regime as a general before being

98. *A statue of Francisco de Miranda, in Fitzroy Street.*

accused of treason and acquitted, then fleeing back to London, where he was generally acknowledged as the leader of all the exiled plotters against Spain, who became members of a secret Masonic lodge he founded. Among his acolytes was the teenage Bernardo O'Higgins (1778-1842), Chilean-born son of the viceroy of Peru, who had been sent to Richmond to complete his education. In 1806 Miranda made an abortive attempt to raise Venezuela in arms but, failing to rally popular support, was forced to return to London once more. In 1810 Simon Bolivar (1783-1830) came to London as the emissary of the revolutionary regime in Venezuela. Taking Miranda as his mentor, he persuaded the older man to return with him to Venezuela, where he was appointed a general in the revolutionary army, assuming dictatorial powers when independence was formally declared on July 5th 1811. When Spanish forces counter-attacked Miranda signed an armistice in July 1812. The other revolutionary leaders, Bolivar included, regarding this as betrayal, thwarted his attempted escape and allowed him to be handed over to the Spanish. Miranda died in chains in a prison in Cadiz. A plaque marks Miranda's former residence at 58 Grafton Way and a statue stands at the junction of Fitzroy Street and Fitzroy Square nearby. Another plaque at 58 Grafton Way commemorates the residence of Miranda's compatriot, Andres Bello (1781-1865), "the intellectual father of South America". A protégé of the German polymath Alexander von Humboldt, Bello lived in London for nineteen years, publishing the first two sections of a projected epic poem, extolling the grandeur of the South American landscape, in 1826-7. Returning to South America Bello founded the University of Chile, wrote a definitive grammar of the Spanish language and drafted a civil law code adopted by Chile, Colombia and Ecuador.

Bernardo O'Higgins played a leading role in the liberation of Chile in collaboration with José de San Martin (1778-1850). Although born in Argentina, San Martin was initially a loyal royalist officer and may have turned his loyalties after passing through London en route to the land of his birth. O'Higgins would become the first ruler – 'supreme director' – of his native Chile in 1817-23. Although he consolidated the revolution by establishing order and the basic structure of a government, he failed to secure a political base and spent his later life in exile in Peru. San Martin, after a decisive meeting with Bolivar, opted to spend the rest of his life in European exile, spending just over two months at 23 Park Road, just by Regent's Park in 1824, en route to the Continent. A statue of San Martin stands in Belgrave Square..

Bolivar became the liberator of Venezuela, Ecuador, Colombia, Peru, Bolivia and Panama but, unable to prevent their fragmentation into separate states, instead of a single Gran Colombia, died believing himself to have been a failure. Although Bolivar was a superb horseman

Hugo Dani's 1974 Belgrave Square statue shows him on foot, clothed in the flamboyant general's uniform he always wore and clutching a written constitution. Bolivar exercised dictatorial power in Peru and Colombia, but like the English-educated O'Higgins, he was an admirer of British constitutionalism. The pedestal of Bolivar's statue bears his declaration that "I am convinced that England alone is capable of protecting the world's precious rights as she is great, glorious and wise." A plaque marks the house at 4 Duke Street, Marylebone which was Bolivar's London residence.

The Spanish

Traditionally an enemy of Britain, Catholic Spain became an ally as a result of Napoleon's determination to overrun the Iberian peninsula. The aftermath of Spanish liberation was, however, political confusion as the liberal constitution promulgated in 1812 was overthrown by a military coup in 1814, restoring Ferdinand VII to the throne as an absolutist. Overthrown in turn in 1820, Ferdinand was restored by French military intervention in 1823. Liberal opponents of absolutism fled, some to London, where they were seen by Thomas Carlyle – "you could see a group of fifty or a hundred stately tragic figures, in proud threadbare cloaks; perambulating … the broad pavements of Euston Square and the regions about St. Pancras new Church. Their lodging was chiefly in Somers Town … and those open pavements about St. Pancras church were the general place of rendezvous. They spoke little or no English; knew nobody, could employ themselves on nothing …". The Carlist wars of 1833-40 and 1848 produced new waves of refugees, as Carlyle noted in 1851, musing on the fate of those he had seen a quarter of a century previously –

"That particular Flight of Unfortunates has long since fled again, and vanished; and new have come and fled. In this convulsed revolutionary epoch, which already lasts above fifty years, what tragic flights of such have we not seen arrive on the one safe coast which is open to them, as they get successively vanquished and chased into exile to avoid worse! Swarm after swarm, of ever new complexion, from Spain as from other countries ...".

The Italians

During the nineteenth century the frequent reverses in the movement for Italian unification and freedom from foreign rule brought many exiles to London. Poet Ugo Foscolo (1778-1827) fled Milan when it was occupied by the Austrians in 1814. He lived briefly in comfort in Edwardes Square, Kensington before ultimately dying in poverty. Half a century later his body was repatriated for a state funeral.

Involvement in the conspiratorial movement known as the Carbonari caused Gabriele Rossetti (1783-1854) to flee from Naples to London in 1824. He became the first Professor of Italian at King's College, London and was the father of the muse of the Pre-Raphaelites, poet-painter, Dante Gabriel Rossetti and of poet Christina Rossetti.

Genoese-born Giuseppe Mazzini (1805-72), another member of the Carbonari, lived more of his life abroad than in his native land, remaining doggedly dedicated to revolutionary republicanism.

A child prodigy who had entered university at fourteen, he had practised as a poor man's lawyer, dabbled in journalism and dreamed of literary fame. Betrayed, imprisoned, then exiled by 1837 he was in London where he set up

schools to help the children of Italian immigrants keep up their language and published a populist newspaper for the Italian community. Mazzini returned to Italy in 1848, serving briefly under Garibaldi, and returning to London in disgust at the monarchist tendency of the emerging movement for national unification. In 1849 he went back to head a short-lived Roman republic but was back in London again by 1851. Founding a group called the Friends of Italy he plotted further abortive uprisings and dressed perpetually in mourning for the occupation and division of his country. Another brief period of service under Garibaldi in 1860 was followed by another return to London. In 1870 Mazzini left London for the last time to head yet another abortive republican uprising in Sicily. Italy was finally united in that same year, to his disgust under a monarchy. Mazzini is commemorated by handsome bronze plaques, sadly obscured by grime, at 183 North Gower Street and at 10 Laystall Street, Clerkenwell and 5 Hatton Garden in what was once the heart of Victorian London's

100. Giuseppe Mazzini.

99. Ugo Foscolo's residence in South Bank, St John's Wood.

manifesto illustrates, is over two centuries old. In 1852 Aleksandr Herzen (1812-70), who sought a uniquely Russian path to socialism, settled in London and, with the help of Polish exiles, founded the 'Free Russian Press in London", the first uncensored printing-press in Russian history. This produced a series of periodicals to be smuggled back into Russia, notably *Kolokol* (*The Bell*) which was read not only by the revolutionary opposition but by the Tsar's own ministers as well.

Former Tsarist bureaucrat Prince Peter Kropotkin (1842-1921) first came to London in 1881 to attend an International Anarchist Congress. He settled in Whitechapel in 1887 and was to remain in Britain until the revolution of 1917 enabled him to return home.

Lenin lived in London for two extended periods and, in the former Welsh school at Clerkenwell Green, later and very appropriately, the home of the Marx Memorial Library, was able to produce his subversive news-sheet, *Iskra* (*The Spark*). Moved on from Brussels by the police, in 1903 Lenin, Trotsky, Stalin and Gorky were allowed to convene in London as participants in a Second Congress of revolutionary Marxists, a gathering which famously led the somewhat mis-named Russian Social Democrats to split into Bolsheviks and Mensheviks.

So long as revolutionism was confined to words, spoken or written, it was by and large tolerated. Violent criminal behaviour was not. In December 1910 an armed gang of Latvian anarchists attracted the attention of the City of London police as they attempted to break into a jeweller's shop in Houndsditch. Three policemen were killed and two seriously wounded as the robbers escaped. Early in January supposed members of the gang, including its leader Peter Piatkow ('Peter the Painter') were cornered in a house in Sidney Street, Stepney. Home Secretary Winston Churchill controversially called in a detachment of Scots Guards from the Tower to take on the gunmen, two of whom perished as the house caught fire. Peter the Painter was never found. Another alleged member of the gang, Jacob Peters, was acquitted and eventually

103. Peter Piatkow – 'Peter the Painter', who disappeared from the Siege of Sidney Street.

returned to Russia to become deputy head of the Communist secret political police, the Cheka.

Brotherhood of Man

London's self-image as the centre of the world was periodically affirmed by celebratory occasions which asserted Britain's global supremacy. In June 1897 Queen Victoria's Diamond Jubilee was organised as a distinctively imperial occasion. The newly-founded *Daily Mail* struck a characteristic note in exulting that the royal procession through London was "escorted by representatives of the greatest Empire the world has ever known ... an

104. *The Siege of Sidney Street in 1910. Churchill brought in Scots Guards to try to flush out the Latvian anarchists.*

anthropological museum ... a living gazetteer ... How small you must feel in the face of the stupendous whole and yet how great to be a unit in it!" The *New York Times* was moved to claim that Americans too, were "a part, and a great part, of the Greater Britain, which seems so plainly destined to dominate this planet." Beatrice Webb noted sourly in her diary "Imperialism in the air, all classes drunk with sightseeing and hysterical loyalty." A decade later Empire Day was instituted as an annual ritual in London's schools.

If necessarily less celebratory the funerals of Victoria and Edward VII also demonstrated how Britain's ruling house could command the homage of lesser realms.

A quite novel feature was added to the London scene by the construction of a permanent international exhibition centre, the White City at Shepherd's Bush. An exotic confection created by Hungarian impresario Imre Kiralfy, in 1908 it was used to accommodate an 'exposition' celebrating the renewal of the Anglo-French diplomatic Entente-Cordiale. At the same time, on an adjacent site, London showed that it could manage not one but two *grands projets* simultaneously by building the world's first purpose-built Olympic stadium to host the fourth Olympiad – at which Britain took more medals than all the other competing nations added together. Subsequent exhibitions at the White City celebrated the Anglo-Japanese alliance and Anglo-American ties.

The outbreak of war in 1914 was to reveal that London's cosmopolitanism had severe limits. Rabid xenophobia drove thousands of Germans and Austrians, many settled for decades, to flee. Foreign-owned properties were attacked and looted, including many owned by naturalized Jews from Eastern Europe who had failed to anglicise their names. Ironically some Germans saved themselves from molestation by claiming to be Belgian refugees.

Lest we Forget

The unprecedented slaughter of the Great War was matched by an outburst of memorialisation on a similarly unprecedented scale. In 1919 Sir Edwin Lutyens' hastily devised a temporary national monument for a victory march-past on Whitehall – a single, severely sculpted block of Portland stone, surmounted by a symbolic coffin. The maquette for this original design can still be seen in the Imperial War Museum at Lambeth, which itself opened the following year as another tribute to 'the Fallen'. The striking impression made by Lutyens' design led to its erection as a permanent monument, the Cenotaph (from the Greek for 'empty tomb'). As part of the same ceremony the burial of an Unknown Warrior in Westminster Abbey was attended by an honour guard of a hundred holders of the Victoria Cross. The same year witnessed the unveiling of a monument to Nurse Edith Cavell, who was shot as a spy by the Germans while aiding British soldiers to escape from Belgium. One of Sir George Frampton's less happy compositions, it stands opposite the National Portrait Gallery.

Lutyens' memorial to the twelve thousand lost at sea from the merchant marine and fishing fleets takes the form of a Doric temple at Tower Hill.

The Royal Artillery memorial at Hyde Park Corner made the reputation of Charles Sargeant Jagger (grandfather of the rock musician, Mick Jagger), creator of its brooding bronzes; the howitzer, zeroed in to the battlefields of Flanders and the supporting plinth, incised with scenes of action, was the work of Lionel Pearson. The nearby monument to the Machine Gun Corps is a bronze nude of David with a sword and the chilling inscription "Saul hath slain his thousands, but David his tens of thousands". The Cavalry Memorial, St. George slaying the dragon, was moved to Hyde Park in 1961 but originally (1924) stood at Stanhope Gate. The sculptor, Adrian Jones, was himself a cavalryman.

At Horse Guards Parade a chunky obelisk, inscribed with the names of dozens of battle honours, testifies to the valour of the Brigade of Guards.

Outside the Ministry of Defence stands a statue of Lord Trenchard, creator of the RAF. On

105. *The Cavell monument near St Martin-in-the-Fields.*

the river bank opposite a golden eagle on a stone plinth stands for the RAF itself; designed by Sir Reginald Blomfield it was executed by Sir William Reid Dick. Further along the Embankment are memorials to the Camel Corps, Belgian refugees to Britain and Submariners.

At Chancery Lane a Royal Fusilier sergeant commemorates the loss of 22,000 men of London's own regiment. Nearby in the courtyard of the Prudential building a fallen soldier is borne heavenwards by angels from a plinth on which are inscribed the names of over a thousand of the company's employees. Men recruited from the Midland Bank are remembered in the foyer of its

106. *The Royal Artillery memorial at Hyde Park Corner, the work of Charles Jagger and Lionel Pearson.*

107. *The Guards' Memorial at Horse Guards Parade, sculpted by A. Chalton Bradshaw.*

110. *Part of the vast Becontree Estate, the most ambitious of the LCC's housing projects, built without regard to the availability of jobs or transport facilities.*

'Freedom' from the slums was bought at the cost of amenity and community. While many relished the chance to cultivate their own patch of garden others chafed at a maintenance regime which laid down detailed rules about even the condition of door-hinges. In the first decade of Becontree's existence no less than a third of its new residents voted against it by leaving of their own accord.

Planners had envisaged not just a garden suburb but "a township more or less complete in itself". But they hadn't even thought about jobs. Were the newcomers expected to throng back to the docks and workshops of the East End daily? If so, it was a pity that, although extra-wide roads had been laid out for trams the tram services never materialised beyond Barking. It was sheer coincidence that the Ford Motor Company decided to create a massive motor-manufacturing plant at Dagenham Dock. And at first the authorities even refused accommodation to key Ford workers from Manchester because meeting their housing needs had not been part of the original intent. Schools were another oversight. There weren't any new ones and church halls had to be pressed into service until there were. As Prime Minister Stanley Baldwin ruefully observed in 1934 there was more to housing than providing houses.

The LCC's second biggest 'out county' project was the Watling Estate of 1926-30, built to the north of Burnt Oak station on the Northern Line, which opened in 1924. The 1921 population of 1,000 had become 21,545 ten years later. War veteran and veteran stall-holder Jack Cohen seized the opportunity to open London's first Tesco grocery store there in 1929. The residents of the four thousand new homes were stigmatised by their neighbours as breeders of a feral race of petty thieves and vandals and their community branded 'Little Moscow'. It is now a conservation area.

Poplarism

As one of London's poorest boroughs Poplar was hit particularly hard by the rising unemployment of the unanticipated postwar slump. In August 1921, when there were 62,000 dockworkers registered as available; the highest number working on any one day was 29,000. By 1922 when fewer than one in twenty people in England and Wales was in receipt of poor relief, in Poplar the figure was one in five. Relief scales in Poplar were above those of most other Boards of Guardians and set no maximum for a family, so families with very many children could actually be better off on relief. The leading personality of Poplar's Labour council, George Lansbury *(see p. 170)*, had refused "to tax the poor to help the poor" and from March 1921 had in effect ordered the distribution as relief of that portion of local rates which should have been forwarded to the LCC and other London-wide bodies to cover Poplar's assessed share of the costs of providing policing, fire brigade services and asylums. By doing so Lansbury drew attention to the injustice of a system whereby the poorest boroughs, suffering the highest rates of unemployment, were expected to bear the greatest burden of poor relief while least able to do so. In July 1921 the government took Poplar Council before the High Court and as a result thirty Poplar councillors were imprisoned, the men in Brixton, the women in Holloway. Huge crowds turned out to cheer them on their way to their confinement. Council meetings continued to be convened in prison, the women councillors being ferried over to Brixton by taxi. Stepney and Bethnal Green followed Poplar's lead and refused to levy rates for the outside precepting bodies. After six weeks the rate rebels were released without having "purged their contempt". The hasty establishment of a pooled Metropolitan Common Poor Fund conceded their principal demand that the burden of relief should be shared more fairly between richer and poorer boroughs. When the Poplar Guardians continued to pay its 29,000 recipients above the maximum set by the new Fund an official enquiry denounced its failure to force the able-bodied to

111. *George Lansbury.*

work in return for relief or to discriminate between the 'deserving' and 'undeserving'. It also revealed that the Guardians' Relief Committee had in addition distributed 13,245 pairs of free boots over the course of a year, as well as unmarked second-hand clothing which "could be pawned or sold without chance of detection." Even those who had been falsely claiming relief while actually earning had not been prosecuted, merely being warned and having their relief cancelled. The 800 inmates of the Poplar Workhouse, moreover, were being treated as though the institution was more "an almshouse than a workhouse", where butter had replaced margarine in the official dietary scales at an extra cost of £600 a year. Of Poplar's annual relief expenditure of £229,000 it was recommended that £100,000 a year should be cut. The Guardians responded with a pamphlet cheerily entitled *Guilty and Proud of It*, stating

No Anarchy Please, We're British

Perhaps the most telling observation that can be made regarding anarchism and anarchists in Britain is the fact that Butler and Butler's *Twentieth Century British Political Facts 1900-2000* (8th edition 2000) – "the definitive record of the who, the what and the when of British political history" – contains not a single reference to either. Nor do they appear in *Cassell's Companion to Twentieth Century Britain,* or *The London Encyclopaedia* and other reference works.

That said, a foretaste of anarchism in its utopian mode can be seen in the Diggers' abortive attempt to create an agrarian collective by occupying St. George's Hill, Weybridge in 1649. Spence *(see p. 69)* envisaged the hierarchy of government rising no further than the parish level. Godwin *(see p. 70)* went further, denouncing government as the inherently brutal oppressor and corrupter of mankind. The botched Cato Street conspiracy of 1820 (see p. 79) conformed more closely to the popular conception of anarchism in action, though it can scarcely be claimed to have had any considered theoretical basis. The same might be said of the Baltic gangsters whose criminal career was terminated at the Siege of Sidney Street *(see p. 132)*.

In the late nineteenth century anarchism did find a lodgement in the East End, though its origins and appeal were both inherently alien. In 1886 Peter Kropotkin, with the backing of William Morris, founded the Freedom Press, whose complex, roller-coaster history has included spells of inactivity and relocation to the Cotswolds, but is claimed to be the oldest surviving anarchist publishing house in the world.

The Scottish-born German Henry Mackay (1864-1933) based his autobiographical novel *The Anarchists: A Picture of Civilization at the Close of the Nineteenth Century* (1891) partly on his own contacts with East End anarchists in 1887-88. Local journalist Arthur Morrison's novel *Tales of Mean Streets* (1894) includes an account of an anarchist band. Anarchists also figure in the short stories of George R. Sims. The death of a supposed anarchist bomber in Greenwich Park supplied the inspiration for Joseph Conrad's novel *The Secret Agent* (1907).

Rudolf Rocker (1873-1958), a German Catholic by birth, settled in the East End in 1895 and became the central figure of a group of anarchists which met at the Sugar Loaf in Hanbury Street, Spitalfields and later at the Alexandra Hall in Jubilee Street.

Other members of the group included Kropotkin and Errico Malatesta (1853-1932). As editor of the Yiddish-medium *Der Arbeter Fraint* – unlike the establishment of Anglo-Jewry, which insisted on Anglophone competence – Rocker cherished Yiddish as the *mameloshn*, the mother tongue and common heritage of the working masses.

The Freedom Press was effectively re-established in 1936 by Vernon Richards (1915-2001), born Vero Recchioni in Soho, the son of an Italian anarchist who had escaped the island prison of Pantelleria, managed a celebrated delicatessen, King Bomba, and plotted to assassinate Mussolini. In 1936 Richards began to produce *Spain and the World* to give an English-language view of the anarchist side of the Spanish civil war. The Freedom Press became based in Whitechapel and at various times produced *War Commentary* (1939-45), the anarchist newspaper *Freedom*, the monthly *Anarchy* and a prolific output of pamphlets, anthologies, reprints and original titles. Since 1968 Freedom Press and its bookshop have been in Angel Alley, 84b Whitechapel High Street, where its premises were firebombed in 1994. Working variously as manager of the family deli, a railway engineer, freelance photographer, travel courier and organic farmer, Richards edited *Freedom* until 1964 and wrote for it until the 1990s.

Self-styled 'anarchists' of the 'rentamob' variety formed a significant element in the anti-poll tax, 'anti-capitalist' and 'anti-globalisation' riots which surprised the forces of order in post-Thatcher London. Their participation was sufficient to confirm the validity of Professor John Cannon's astute observation that "fear of anarchy, an important ingredient of the conservative tradition, was always in Britain more influential than anarchism itself."

that this had been an error, never subsequently finding a position that 'stretched' him as satisfyingly. From 1940 to 1942 he served in Churchill's war Cabinet as Minister of Information, then Minister of Transport, then Minister of Works. Reith lived modestly in the corner house on Cowley Street in the shadow of Parliament. The prestigious Reith Lectures, named in his honour, were instituted in 1948.

Showcase of Empire

As the mood of national grief faded it was replaced by a desire for a gesture of national self-confidence. The result was the opening in 1923 of a major new football stadium at Wembley which became the adjunct to the British Empire Exhibition the following year. At one level an assertion of "the wondrous reality of Britain's might and magnitude, her grandeur and her glory", it also served, as the Prince of Wales, himself an unemployed veteran of the trenches,

observed, as a useful make-work scheme for some twelve thousand men. Funded on a shoe-string budget, the exhibition showcased exhibits from fifty-six countries and was so successful that it was extended into 1925, attracting a final total of 27,000,000 visitors. It failed, however, to become the permanent 'Imperial City' its organisers had originally envisaged.

The General Strike

The General Strike of 1926 proved to be a turning-point at which political history refused to turn, a potentially revolutionary situation which simply went off the boil. The origins of the largest confrontation faced by any inter-war government lay in the problems of the coal industry. The demands of the war-effort had led to maximum extraction at the expense of under-investment which, when the mines were returned to private ownership, left the industry vulnerable to overseas competition. The mine-owners were

114. The new Wembley stadium opened in 1923 with an FA Cup Final between West Ham and Bolton. It descended into dangerous chaos when the stadium was invaded by those who had no tickets. Order was famously restored by a policeman on a white horse.

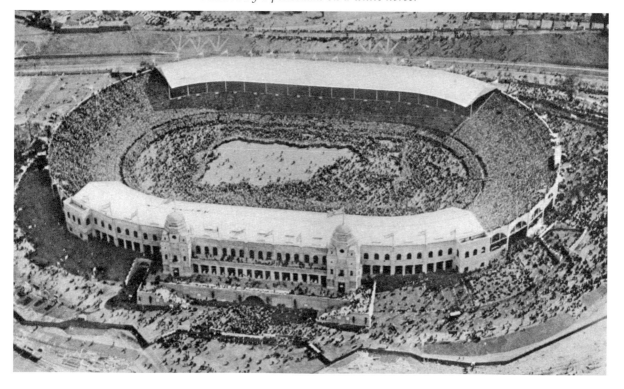

115 & 116. *Two scenes during the General Strike of 1926. Above, a corner of Hyde Park is being used as a temporary milk depot. Below, a bus is being towed away by a lorry after its volunteer bus driver was attacked by strikers.*

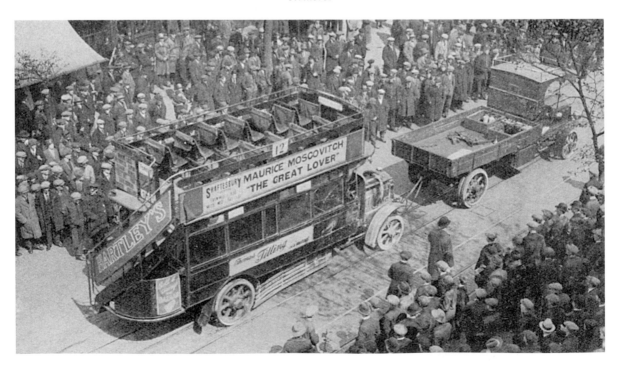

convinced that their labour-intensive operations could only be returned to profitability through wage-reductions, which the miners were equally determined to resist. The miners' preferred solution was nationalisation as the necessary condition for long-overdue rationalisation to eliminate inefficient pits and make renewed investment economically feasible. For years conflict was postponed by the granting of a government subsidy. When this was finally withdrawn the miners turned to the TUC for support. Meanwhile the government of Stanley Baldwin (1867-1947), presciently apprehensive of an industrial dispute turning into a more general challenge to its authority, recruited volunteers for an Organisation for the Maintenance of Supplies to minimise the disruption that any withdrawal of labour on a mass-scale would inevitably bring about. Many OMS volunteers were ex-servicemen, mobilised through Earl Haig's recently established veterans' association, the British Legion.

The TUC by contrast made only belated and half-hearted preparations. The miners having refused a 13% pay cut and the imposition of a standard eight-hour day at the coal-face, negotiations were conducted on their behalf at Cabinet level by a TUC team. On May 3rd compositors on the *Daily Mail*, on their own initiative and without the knowledge of the TUC, refused to set the type for an anti-Union editorial, thus handing the government the opportunity to misrepresent their action as an attack on the freedom of the press and thus on constitutional government itself. Despite the studied moderation of most strikers throughout the dispute, despite the fact that thousands wore their war medals to demonstrate their proven patriotism, Baldwin did not hesitate to equate the strikers with traitors – "The General Strike is a challenge to Parliament and is the road to anarchy and ruin".

The bemused leaders of the TUC thus found themselves in a crisis which they had not sought and for which they had scarcely prepared. They responded by calling out organised labour in tranches while carefully refusing to interfere

with the normal distribution of milk, medicines and food, sanitation, the generation of electrical power for non-industrial uses, the delivery of post, the building of schools or hospitals or the functioning of the retail sector. By the end of the dispute some 2,000,000 workers had answered the call to support the miners' cause by withdrawing their labour.

The most clearly visible impact of the strike was the disappearance of newspapers and the virtual cessation of public transport. Of London's 4,400 buses only about forty continued in service, of its 2,000 trams only nine. London cabbies also supported the strike. The government riposted provocatively by arranging for convoys of supplies to be brought along the East India Dock Road under the ostentatious and entirely superfluous escort of armoured cars. A food distribution depot was established in Hyde Park, where 'Society' ladies cooked for its volunteer staff. Others worked the tea urns at a Scotland Yard Special Constables' Canteen.

Baldwin's government filled the news vacuum by creating its own newspaper, *The British Gazette*, a broadsheet format newsletter which could be pasted up like a poster. Baldwin himself later asserted that its chief value was to give his belligerent colleague, Winston Churchill, something to do rather than being free to antagonise the strikers. Churchill himself relished the challenge of inventing a newspaper from scratch, which he likened to a cross between fighting an election and running a battleship. Commandeering the presses of the *Daily Express* and drumming up a skeleton staff of press managers, Churchill achieved a print-run of 2,500,000 copies, though most of these never got distributed beyond the deserted railway and Underground stations where they were optimistically dumped in piles. The TUC created its own organ, *The British Worker*, produced by the staff of the *Daily Herald*. Even *The Times* acknowledged it as "a straightforward and moderating influence". Like the *British Gazette* the TUC's mouthpiece failed to achieve effective distribution. Many jobbing printers seized the chance to churn out their own news-sheets, often

A Suitable Address

While 'Political London' might at first thought simply be equated with Westminster and Whitehall, further reflection suggests many other particular locations strongly associated with significant institutions and events or the mere presence of the powerful. Here are just a few.

St. James's Square

Architecturally speaking St. James's Square was the point of departure from which the surrounding court suburb developed. It owed its origins to an act of straightforward political cronyism when, in 1665, Charles II granted a freehold to his favourite Henry Jermyn, Earl of St. Albans, to build a square "fit for the dwellings of Noblemen and Persons of Quality."

Now dominated by an equestrian statue of William III, St. James's Square has over the three and a half centuries since then enjoyed very various associations with Britain's political life. James II's mistress, Arabella Churchill, was once a resident. Ernest Bevin, architect of NATO, came here to attend YMCA evening classes. In 1984 a demonstration outside No. 5, the Libyan Arab Republic People's Bureau (i.e. embassy), led one of its occupants to shoot dead duty officer WPC Yvonne Fletcher and thus led to the breaking-off of diplomatic relations between Britain and Libya. The memorial near where she fell is never without a tribute of flowers.

By the 1720s St. James's Square was home to seven dukes and seven earls. Sir Robert Walpole lived at No. 32 from 1732 to 1735, when he moved to become the first occupant of No. 10 Downing Street as the official residence of the Prime Minister. From 1771 until 1919 No. 32

119. St James's Square, a view by Sutton Nicholls, c.1722.

belonged to the bishops of London. Other eighteenth-century residents included at various times ambassadors from France, Austria, Sweden, Venice and the Netherlands.

William Pitt the Elder was living at No. 10 in 1759 when he received news of the capture of Quebec, which wrested control of Canada from French to British rule. In 1815, at a ball at No. 16, the Prince Regent learned of Wellington's victory over Napoleon at Waterloo. The blood-stained courier, Major Henry Percy, who emerged from a carriage bearing captured French colours, was promoted to the rank of a full Colonel on the spot. From 1815 until 1822 No. 18 was the home of Foreign Secretary, Lord Castlereagh, until he slashed his throat there for fear of being exposed as a homosexual.

By the 1850s the square had lost its aristocratic tone. Although it was home to three gentlemen's clubs and two government offices and the London Library; there were also two lodging-houses, a bank and an insurance company. Another turn-about came with the occupation of No. 10 by two Prime Ministers, Lord Derby and W.E. Gladstone. After World War One the house became home to the Royal Institute of International Affairs.

No. 20 was the childhood home of Queen Elizabeth, the Queen Mother. Nancy Astor, the first woman MP to take her seat, occupied No. 4, now the Naval and Military Club, from 1912 to 1942, entertaining guests as varied as Gandhi, Lindbergh and Ribbentrop. Norfolk House, for generations the London residence of the Dukes of Norfolk and birthplace of George III, was sold off on the eve of World War Two and was occupied by General Eisenhower while planning the invasions of North Africa, Operation Torch, and Normandy, Operation Overlord.

Queen Anne's Gate

This exquisite street was originally two separate closes, separated by a wall until 1873. The western part, originally known as Queen Square, dates from *ca.*1704-5, many of the houses retaining their imposing wooden door canopies. The eastern part, formerly Park Street, was laid out *ca.* 1686 but re-built in the late eighteenth century, Nos. 6-12 being added in the 1830s.

No. 40 (then No. 1 Queen Square) was owned

120.   Queen Anne's Gate when divided by an iron railing (which replaced a brick wall) in 1850. Watercolour by T H Shepherd. Except for the railing, it has hardly changed today.

by Jeremy Bentham and let by him to James Mill, who occupied it from 1814 to 1831 for a rental of £50 per year. It was, therefore, the boyhood home of John Stuart Mill. Blue plaques proclaim the birthplace of Lord Palmerston (No.20) and the former residences of Lord Haldane (No.28), creator of the Territorial Army, Foreign Secretary and avid ornithologist Sir Edward Grey (No.3) and Admiral 'Jacky' Fisher, architect of the Dreadnought battleship programme (No16), whose house was previously occupied by William Smith, a Foxite opponent of the wars with France. No. 9 was once the home of the top-hatted imperialist and socialist pioneer H.M. Hyndman.

British Army Intelligence was housed at Nos.16-18 between 1884 and 1901. Robert Baden-Powell, founder of the Boy Scouts, reported there having posed as a butterfly-collector while covertly sketching fortifications in Dalmatia. No. 21 was the home of Admiral Mansfield Smith-Cumming, the first chief of MI6, after whose initial and practice all subsequent chiefs were known as 'C' and privileged to write in green ink.

Institutional occupants of the street have included the Director of Public Prosecutions, the UK Office of the European Parliament and the National Trust.

Eaton Square

Quite possibly the most expensive address in London, Eaton Square marks the entrance to swanky Belgravia, the core of the Duke of Westminster's Grosvenor Estate and a favoured location for major embassies. Built between 1826 and 1855, Eaton Square is actually bisected by the King's Road, flanked by exclusive gardens, open only to residents.

The arch-conservative Austrian Chancellor, Prince Metternich (1773-1859) found refuge at 44 Eaton Square when chased into exile by revolutionaries in 1848. The aged Duke of Wellington made a point of calling on him more than once but Metternich found the locality too expensive and was forced to find other accommodation. In 1922 Field Marshal Sir Henry Wilson was assassinated on the doorstep of his Eaton Square home by two IRA gunmen, having just returned from unveiling a war memorial to the men of the LNER at Liverpool Street station. No. 93 was the home of Stanley Baldwin between 1920 and 1923, when he unexpectedly became Prime Minister. No. 37 was the home of Neville Chamberlain from 1923 until 1935, during which period he was Minister of Health (1924-9) and, for the second time, Chancellor of the Exchequer (1931-7). No. 86 was the home of Lord Halifax (1881-1959), Chamberlain's Foreign Secretary and Churchill's rival for the premiership in 1940. Tory backbench MP and latterly a populist broadcaster Lord Robert 'Bob' Boothby lived at No. 1 for forty years. No. 112 was the home of the Amery dynasty of Conservative politicians from 1924 onwards. No. 42 was the home of Peter, Lord Thorneycroft (1905-94) who served as Chancellor of the Exchquer, first Secretary of State for Defence and as, Chairman of the Conservative Party, was credited with a major role in the election campaign which brought Margaret Thatcher to power in 1979.

Lord North Street

Dating from 1722 this short, quiet Pimlico side-street survives virtually complete. It was named North Street until 1937, when the desire of the LCC to minimise the duplication of street names led to a posthumous compliment to the Prime Minister who lost the American colonies. During the nineteenth century the houses were split up into tenements but the street began to recover its standing when Sir Stuart Samuel MP, President of the Board of Jewish Deputies, moved into No. 2, now the home of the Institute of Economic Affairs.

Labour Prime Minister Harold Wilson lived at No. 5 in 1974-76. From 1933 until 1958 No. 8 was the home of Brendan Bracken (1901-58), wartime Minister of Information and subsequently editor of the *Financial Times*. No. 8 later became the home of disgraced Tory MP Jonathan Aitken, at one time tipped to become a future Prime Minister. No. 11 served as the base from which Michael Portillo and Iain Duncan Smith ran their respective bids for the Tory leadership in 1995 and 2001 respectively. No. 16 was the home of the Marchioness of Reading, founder of Women's

Royal Voluntary Service. No. 19, last home of the socialite and interior decorator Lady Sibyl Colefax, a niece of Walter Bagehot, was later occupied by Edward Du Cann, chairman of the Tory 1922 Committee, and after him by Tory Chief Whip Alistair Goodlad. C.P. Snow was therefore quite right to make Lord North Street the home of Tory MP Roger Quaife in *Corridors of Power*. In 2007 the rental on a five-storey house in Lord North Street was £7,000 a month.

Dolphin Square

When it was built in 1937 Dolphin Square in Pimlico was claimed to be the largest self-contained apartment complex in Europe. The various blocks are all named after British admirals. Over fifty MPs have been residents, including Labour politicians Arthur Greenwood (1880-1954), 'Red Ellen' Wilkinson (1891-1947) and left-winger Eric Heffer (1922-91). During World War Two Ida and Louise Cook used a Dolphin Square flat as a refuge for Jews whom they had helped to escape from Nazi-occupied territories. Ida, a prolific author for Mills & Boon became founder and President of the Romantic Writers' Association and was honoured by Israel as a 'Righteous Gentile' for her work for refugees. 10 Collingwood House was used by MI5 officer Maxwell Knight (1900-80) to recruit agents who included the Labour MP Tom Driberg and the spy novelist John Le Carre.

In 1962 a raid on 308 Hood House, formerly used as a safe house by Maxwell Knight and at the time the home of Admiralty clerk John Vassall (1924-96), uncovered 140 classified documents, which secured his conviction as a Soviet spy. Vassall presumably had a hard time explaining how out of his salary of £14 a week he was able to afford £10 for rent and a wardrobe containing 19 Savile Row suits.

Hampstead

Hampstead has become virtually synonymous with 'intellectual' and was indeed the chosen home of Freud, the Huxley family, John Galsworthy and Professor Nikolaus Pevsner, the doyen of architectural historians. It would normally be assumed that the *bien-pensant* residents of 'the Village' lean to the Left but Pitt the Elder once lived in a house in what is now North End Avenue, though all that survives is his name on the current Pitt House. The eminent judge, Lord Mansfield, whose Bloomsbury residence was sacked by the Gordon rioters *(see p. 57)*, had his rural retreat at Kenwood, which, with its superb grounds and fine art collection, survives as one of the architectural and cultural treasures of London.

Liberal Prime Minister Herbert Asquith lived at 27 Maresfield Gardens. But the presumption of Hampstead's left-wing sympathies would not be incorrect. Karl Marx himself lived the last eight years of his life and died in the respectable villadom of Maitland Park Road. Sidney and Beatrice Webb *(see p. 107)* began their married lives at 10 Netherhall Gardens. No. 51 in the same road was the home of John Passmore Edwards (1823-1911). Most remembered for his philanthropy in funding public libraries, parks and galleries, Edwards was a campaigning newspaper proprietor who doughtily championed a range of controversial and unpopular causes, from the abolition of flogging and capital punishment to the suppression of gambling and the opium trade. 13 Well Walk was the home of H.M. Hyndman (1842-1921) the truculent leader of the Social Democratic Federation from 1916 until his death.

Britain's first Labour Prime Minister Ramsay MacDonald (1866-1937) also moved to Hampstead in 1916, occupying 9 Howitt Road until his move to 10 Downing Street. Following his brief tenure of the premiership he returned in 1925 to considerably more imposing surroundings at 103 Frognal, which remained his home until his death. In 1934-5 George Orwell worked in a bookshop, long gone, on Pond Street. His home was at 77 Parliament Hill. Hugh Gaitskell (1906-63), Attlee's successor as leader of the Labour Party lived at 18 Redington Road and lies buried in the churchyard of the parish church of St. John-at-Hampstead. The undeniably cerebral Michael Foot, another Labour Party leader, albeit even less likely to have become Prime Minister, is, at the time of writing, the doyen of Hampstead's leftist intellectuals.

CHAPTER TEN

Finest Hour

Starter's Orders

In a speech made as early as 1934 Winston Churchill warned Londoners that "We cannot move London ... the flying peril is not a peril from which we can fly ...". Thanks to London's suburban building boom the metropolitan area doubled in size in the inter-war period to create an unmissable target of four hundred square miles.

Cinema-going Londoners who saw the film version of H.G. Wells' *Things to Come* in 1936 could have been left in little doubt about the carnage that aerial bombing could inflict on the civilians of a defenceless city. If they were they should have been set straight by the newsreel footage that would later reach their screens from Spain's civil war and Japan's invasion of China, with the bombing of the Basque town of Guernica in April 1937 and of Shanghai in August of the same year. Yet when the government passed an Air Raid Precautions Act in 1937 its call for civil defence volunteers raised only fifty per cent of the numbers required. It took the Munich crisis of September 1938 to awaken Londoners to the threat menacing their homes. Gas masks were distributed at local police stations. Pamphlets were dropped through letter-boxes to inform householders how to prepare their homes and families against the expected effects of aerial warfare. The LCC organised a practice evacuation of four thousand children, from which many valuable lessons were learned.

The outbreak of war was formally announced by Prime Minister Neville Chamberlain, broadcasting from the Cabinet Room at No. 10. Speaking on a Sunday morning he could be heard by most Londoners as they sat in their own living-rooms. More than half a million of the city's children had already been evacuated over the previous week, apparently without serious mishap to any, though amidst much confusion about where they had actually gone. The city's greatest artistic treasures had been stripped out over previous months, consigned to safe storage in Welsh slate quarries, provincial prisons and rural stately homes. A complete nightly blackout was strictly enforced, at the cost of some forty fatalities a day as Londoners blundered into and off inadequately marked obstacles and hazards or fell victim to traffic driven with minimal lighting. In the first year of the war almost one Londoner in five suffered some sort of blackout-related accident or injury.

Carefully prepared schemes of rationing for various categories of foodstuff, then clothes and household goods, would be introduced by stages. Combined with income tax at fifty per cent this would eventually cut civilian living-standards to about half their pre-war level. A black market soon emerged, not merely for indulgences like whisky, but for petrol and even such formerly everyday items as lemons. As inhabitants of a great port and centre of commerce Londoners had the edge on countryfolk when it came to ferreting out little luxuries – but the possibilities for poaching for the pot were severely limited.

The Machinery of Government

The Great War had broken out after a century of peace. Its duration was unanticipated. The expansion of government activities was largely a matter of improvisation. The establishment of what became the massive Ministry of Munitions was the hasty response to a scandalous 'shell shortage'. Rationing, when it was introduced towards the end of the war, starting in London, was poorly co-ordinated and unfair. Lessons were learned. When war broke out again in September 1939 no one in authority was under the illusion that it would be "over by Christmas". An adult population, most of whom could remember "the last lot", knew that fighting a modern war on a global scale would means years, not months, of struggle and sacrifice. The fiasco of Munich bought a year's respite not only for rearmament but for the preparation of such programmes as the just and efficient scheme of food rationing, devised by one of the army of academics who would be seconded from the universities to become technocrats, Professor Jack Drummond. Eventually the new wartime Ministry of Food would employ a staff of fifty thousand to keep the nation nutritionally disciplined.

Beneath the pavements of Whitehall a twenty-one room secret bunker complex was prepared in which the Cabinet might meet in the event of sustained bombing. A Map Room provided the central focus of the subterranean warren. A 'hot line' enabling Churchill to communicate directly with President Roosevelt was installed in what was, in effect, little more than a cupboard whose door, as Churchill himself mischievously observed "bore my initials upon it". Many of the bunker staff did, indeed, take it to be the PM's personal lavatory. From this cramped facility a land-line ran beneath St. James's Park and across the West End to the basement of Selfridge's where the massive electric gear necessary to operate the system was installed in what was taken to be one of London's most bomb-proof buildings. Another, even more secret refuge was established out at Dollis Hill. The massive extension to the Admiralty, known as The Citadel, supplied the most visible architectural evidence of these preparations.

Fortress of Freedom
London's ancient boast to be 'the mansion house of liberty' took on a new aspect as the city came to afford a refuge to the governments-in-exile of Axis-occupied states. The Free French occupied 4 Carlton Gardens, 4 St. James's Square and 1 Dorset Square and socialized at the York Minster in Dean Street, Soho, always colloquially known as 'The French House'. French naval headquarters was established at Stafford Place and an officers' club at 2 Lord North Street. General de Gaulle himself was quartered at the Connaught hotel. The Dutch Queen Wilhelmina took up residence at 77 Chester Square. A club, Oranjehaven, was established on the Bayswater Road for Dutchmen who escaped the occupation of their country to join the war effort. The Belgians occupied much of Eaton Square and, having control of the world's only source of uranium, in the Congo, from there organised its supply for the Manhattan Project to produce an atomic bomb. King Haakon VII of Norway headed a government in exile which could draw on the financial returns from the large Norwegian merchant marine which was managed from the Midland Bank building in Leadenhall Street and made a major contribution to the Battle of the Atlantic. A plaque in the Institute of Directors (then the United Services Club) marks 'Norwegian Corner' where the king habitually lunched with his service officers, Norway House being only a few doors away on Cockspur Street. The Poles led, until his death in a plane crash at Gibraltar in 1943, by the charismatic General Sikorski, took over the Rubens Hotel on Buckingham Palace Road. Guests at Claridge's included the kings of Yugoslavia and Greece, Roosevelt's confidential envoy, Harry Hopkins and William J. Donovan head of the Office of Strategic Services, wartime ancestor of the CIA, whose headquarters were nearby at 68 Brook Street. Emperor Haile Selassie of Ethiopia was at the Langham.

Home Guard
When invasion was expected hourly in the summer of 1940 a call for Local Defence Volunteers was issued to men above and below the regular age-cohort for military service of nineteen to forty-one. It was intended that they should compensate for any deficiencies in fitness, equipment or training by using their local

knowledge and improvised weaponry to harass and delay invading forces until regular troops could be deployed to deal with them. Sceptics translated the L.D.V. of the hastily-devised armbands which did duty for a uniform as a prediction that their reaction to any real danger of combat would be 'Look, Duck and Vanish". Happily renamed the Home Guard by Churchill the organization in practice took over many routine security functions, freeing regular forces to concentrate on training and operations. Acting under the threat of imminent invasion many Home Guard volunteers found their first tasks to be taking down road-signs and erecting obstacles on parks or open spaces which might be used as landing-grounds.

London's postal service alone raised eight battalions of men for the Home Guard and London Transport seven while others were raised by public institutions such as the BBC, the University of London and the Palace of Westminster itself. The first member of the Home Guard to be mentioned in despatches was teenage Peter Willeringhaus who was blown off his motor-cycle during a night air-raid but, despite being wounded, ran three-quarters of a mile to deliver a message before collapsing. Author George Orwell, having had recent combat experience in the Spanish Civil War, was appointed a sergeant instructor in the St. John's Wood unit where he nearly killed his attentive audience fumbling a live grenade during a supposed safety demonstration.

Administering Chaos
The Air Raid Precautions Act of 1937 threw responsibility onto local authorities for reducing and repairing the effects of enemy action against the civilian population. The task would be immense. The civil defence services of London alone would eventually number some 200,000 paid and volunteer staff.

As the responsible body for the capital's fire, ambulance, hospital and education services the LCC established an Air Raid Precautions Sub-Committee to supervise planning and preparations for a possible 'national emergency',

when the word war was still, as yet, taboo. By the time of Munich a cadre of instructors in anti-gas measures had been trained and 16,000 hospital beds readied to receive air raid casualties. Half this number had been achieved by clearing mental hospitals of their inmates, much of the rest by the redesignation of children's and fever hospitals and converting Mill Hill public school into a hospital for emergencies. In retrospect these initial arrangements seem cruelly futile. Gas was never used, though that, of course, could not have been predicted with certainty. But, as secret government estimates put the anticipated casualties from a single raid on the capital at 100,000, the provision of beds would have proved disastrously inadequate had this planning assumption been anything like accurate. As it was London's hospitals met all the demands made upon them, despite losses of staff, equipment and buildings, not only in dealing with the victims of aerial warfare but also in coping with the normal medical needs of a population harassed by the hazards of the blackout and disrupted transport and energy supplies. Precautionary measures would also prove effective in preventing feared outbreaks of epidemic disease when large numbers of people were forced to crowd together in public shelters and Underground stations.

The LCC had begun to recruit volunteers for an Auxiliary Fire Service (AFS) to supplement the regular fire brigade establishment of 2,500 men early in 1938. By the time they were needed, over 23,000 men had been taken on and most were fully trained to man the service's 2,000 appliances. In the meantime trench shelters had been hastily dug in London's parks, which were also quarried to fill sandbags. In May 1939 the LCC acquired college buildings at Egham in Surrey to which some 600 of its staff were relocated.

Detailed planning for the evacuation of the capital's children had begun in January 1939 by a specially-constituted evacuation task force staffed by officials from the Ministry of Health and the Board of Education, supported by officers of the LCC. Priority was to be given to the

121. Evacuation of London children in 1939.

evacuation of children under five with their mothers, schoolchildren and the blind. Public transport would be provided to decant a million and a quarter souls into a reception area stretching from the West Country to the Wash.

When war did break out in September 1939 the LCC's Air Raid Precautions Committee was up-graded to become the Emergency Committee and then the Civil Defence and General Purposes Committee. It was empowered to override all other committees in acting on behalf of the authority as a whole. Council meetings were rescheduled to take place monthly instead of weekly and convened at 11.30 a.m. instead of 2.30 p.m. so that members could get home before nightly air raids began.

Initially evacuation continued but when major raids failed to materialize large numbers of wives and children came back to rejoin husbands left behind. The exodus recommenced in June 1940 when the Battle of Britain brought regular aerial combats to the skies over southern England but this time the priority classes were encouraged to make their own arrangements by drawing on free travel vouchers and billeting allowances. The drift of evacuees back to the capital whenever danger seemed to recede remained a recurrent problem, leading to the constant reopening and closing of schools and the inauguration of a Home Tuition Scheme involving 2,000 teachers and 100,000 children.

In a masterly blend of understatement and euphemism the official history of the LCC notes that – "The London children and the residents of the countryside were brought into sudden and closer awareness of each other. The way of life of the slum dwellers was startlingly revealed, giving an added impetus to the movement ... for a planned reconstruction of London so as to provide better living conditions for its citizens."

In reality the impact of the evacuees was far more startling and its implications even more far-reaching. The arrival of hordes of apparently feral, frequently verminous, metropolitan children, often accompanied by mothers seemingly bereft of any domestic skills, much less any of use in the countryside, caused a furore which arose from every region in which they were billeted. Veteran backbencher and diarist Harold Nicolson noted that, a fortnight into the war, with the nation facing the gravest hazards of its long existence, the House of Commons was giving over precious hours to debating the evacuee issue. The revelation of the deprivations afflicting tens of thousands of the very generation for which the war was being fought prompted the rurally-based Women's Institute to establish its own 'Royal Commission' to investigate urban living conditions. Staffed entirely by women and taking expert testimony from female doctors, teachers, welfare officers and council officials, the Institute produced a seminal report, *Our Towns*, whose recommendations were to form the basis of much of post-war welfare state policy and provision.

With the onset of sustained bombing from September 1940 onwards the LCC assumed responsibility for organising casualty clearing stations and ambulance services, dealing with damaged and unsafe buildings and rescuing

129. George Bernard Shaw.

Ayot St. Lawrence in Hertfordshire from 1906 onwards Shaw also kept an apartment at Adelphi Terrace.

George Lansbury (1859-1940)

Born in Suffolk, George Lansbury *(ill. 111)* devoted his life to the East End and to Poplar in particular, serving it as both councillor and mayor. Lansbury's family moved to the East End when he was nine. His education, if disrupted by attendance at numerous schools, at least lasted until he was fourteen but led only to manual labour. Married at twenty-one, Lansbury was fortunate to succeed to his father-in-law's timber yard. After an abortive attempt to settle in Australia, Lansbury became a successful political agent, initially in the Liberal interest before converting to socialism under the influence

of Marx and Morris. By 1892 he had become a leading figure in the Social Democratic Federation, unsuccessfully contesting Walworth (1895) and Bow and Bromley (1900). Charles Booth's 1890s poverty survey refers to Lansbury as the leader of a socialist club in Ford Street – "not such a bad chap, a rare talker." Frustrated in his parliamentary ambitions, Lansbury made solid progress in Poplar politics, serving as a Guardian of the Poor (from 1893), councillor (from 1903) and Member of the LCC (1910-13). He also served on the Royal Commission on the Poor Laws (1905-9), signing the radical minority report.

Finally elected Labour MP for Bow and Bromley in December 1910, Lansbury resigned in 1912 to re-fight and lose his seat in support of women's suffrage, a quixotic gesture which kept him out of the Commons for a decade. In 1913 he was briefly imprisoned after an Albert Hall speech which appeared to condone the suffragettes' arson tactics. In the meantime Lansbury became nationally known as the founder and editor (1912-22) of the *Daily Herald*. Although this became the official organ of the Labour Party Lansbury, re-elected for Poplar, Bow and Bromley in 1922, was excluded from the 1924 Labour government thanks to his role in Poplarism *(see p. 139)*, his resulting brief period of imprisonment and the king's disapproval of his endorsement of Bolshevism, as published in *What I Saw in Russia* (1920). In 1929 Lansbury became Commissioner of Works in the second Labour administration and, as such, was responsible for the establishment of a swimming Lido at the Serpentine in Hyde Park. On the fall of that government in 1931 Lansbury, as the only Cabinet minister to retain his seat, became Leader of the Labour Party, resigning in 1935 in pacifist protest against Labour's robust response to Mussolini's invasion of Ethiopia. A teetotaller and fervent Christian Socialist, Lansbury, "the most lovable figure in modern politics", typically continued to travel by public transport even as a minister of the Crown. His most recent biography is appropriately subtitled "*At the heart of old Labour*".

Lansbury is memorialised by a plaque marking the site of his former home at 39 Bow Road and by the Lansbury estate in Poplar. Built by the LCC as the 'Living Architecture' feature for the 1951 Festival of Britain and advertised by a poster proclaiming "New homes rise from London's ruins", the Lansbury estate was bounded by the East India Dock Road, Chrisp Street, Burdett Road and the Limehouse Cut. Intended to parade the new icons of planning and 'scientific' building methods, the model community featured its own school, church, pub – the Festive Briton – and a pedestrianized shopping zone. The isolation of the estate from the main Festival site on the South Bank proved a major disincentive to the anticipated hordes of visitors. An annual Lansbury Festival was inaugurated in 2001 to mark the estate's fiftieth anniversary.

Clement Richard Attlee (1883-1967)

Barefoot Stepney girl *"Where are you going, Mr. Attlee?"*

Attlee *"I'm going home to tea"*.

Girl *"I'm going home to see if there is any tea."*

130. *The young Clement Attlee.*

Attlee never forgot that exchange – a concise encapsulation of the gap between his own world, in which a comfortable security could be taken for granted, and a parallel world in which nothing except uncertainty could be taken for granted. The future leader of the Labour Party and Prime Minister served a lengthy but invaluable political apprenticeship in the East End, as he readily acknowledged – "I engaged in various forms of social work in east London. The condition of the people in that area as I saw them at close quarters led me to study their causes and to reconsider the assumptions of the social class to which I belonged."

Born into a prosperous London lawyer's family, Attlee was an undistinguished pupil at Haileybury, gained a second in history at Oxford, qualified as a barrister and seemed set for a quietly conventional career in the law. In 1905, however, he visited Haileybury House, the Stepney boys' club supported by his old school.

By 1907 he had become an officer in the club's cadet corps, then became resident manager of the club. In 1908 Attlee joined the Stepney branch of the Independent Labour Party and later became its secretary. An inheritance from Attlee's father then enabled him to take the poorly-paid position of secretary of the university settlement at Toynbee Hall before becoming a lecturer in social administration at the London School of Economics.

During the Great War Attlee served at Gallipoli and in France, was twice wounded and promoted to the rank of major. In 1919 he was co-opted to Stepney Borough Council to serve as mayor and then became first chairman of the Association of London Labour mayors, which he had himself helped to form. In 1922 Attlee became MP for Limehouse and in the same year married and moved away to suburban Essex but remained active in Stepney politics as an alderman until 1927. Never better than a competent public speaker, Attlee was, however, a formidably effective committee man, crisp and even-handed

Independent Labour Party, then the CPGB, despite which he managed to retain the endorsement of the Labour Party and briefly hold the seat of Battersea North in 1922-23. Although deprived of official party recognition in 1924 Saklatvala managed to win back the seat thanks to the local support of Battersea Labour Party and Trades Council. During his five years in the Commons he spoke repeatedly on behalf of Indian independence and worked to improve the conditions of lascar sailors. Losing his seat in 1929, he failed to win re-election elsewhere but remained a popular and admired public speaker.

Born in Cambridge of a Bengali father and Swedish mother R.P. Dutt (1896-1974) joined the ILP as an Oxford undergraduate and was imprisoned for refusing military service in 1916. After taking a brilliant First he was recruited for the Labour Party's Research Department and became a foundation member of the CPGB, contributing the article on Communism to the 1921 edition of the *Encyclopaedia Britannica*. A subtle but unyielding Leninist, Dutt became the CPGB's main ideologue, the author of numerous books, an expert on colonial issues and for over half a century the contributor of an influential review of current affairs to *Labour Monthly*.

Manchester-born Harry Pollitt (1890-1960) became a trained boilermaker before moving to the East End, where he met Sylvia Pankhurst and became a foundation member of the CPGB. Having served a year in prison for sedition in 1925, Pollitt became Secretary of the CPGB in 1929. Essentially a pragmatist, he was passionate in his opposition to fascism and played a leading role in the formation of the International Brigade, visiting it five times in the field. Although loyal to Moscow he was never servile and knew when to ignore Comintern instructions as well as when to obey. Pollitt stood for Parliament six times as a Communist candidate and died unrepentantly loyal to the memory of Stalin.

William Rust (1903-49), born in Camberwell, entered journalism via Sylvia Pankhurst's *Dreadnought*. An early member of the CPGB, he came to prominence through the Young

Communists' League and like his perennial rival, Pollitt, served his year for sedition in 1925. As founding editor of the *Daily Worker* he made it his power-base and against the odds raised it from a mere party news-sheet to the level of a mass-circulation paper. Slavish to Moscow, he commanded neither the affection or respect garnered by Pollitt.

An undeniable product of proletarian Southwark Jack Dash (1907-89) served his political apprenticeship in the NUWM and after a variety of employments, established a personal power-base in the unofficial but influential London Docks Liaison Committee. An intransigent spokesmen for the dockers' cause during the protracted industrial disputes of the 1960s and 1970s, Dash became a familiar figure via the media thanks to a quick Cockney wit and the disarmingly affable manner which disguised his vocation as a dedicated class warrior. Dash was, however, far more than the cheeky chappie the tabloids loved to hate – ex-boxer, ex-soldier, a fireman in the Blitz, a vegetarian and a lover of paintings, music and the history of London – but he was simplistic in his attachment to an intellectually unrefined brand of communism, deftly summarised in the epitaph he composed for himself:

"Here lies Jack Dash
All he wanted was
To separate them from their cash."

Post Imperial

The dramatic changes which have transformed post-war London's demographic and cultural profile have been far less the result of its own politics than of other peoples'.

Apart from London Transport setting up a recruitment office in Barbados London as such took no initiatives to promote settlement from abroad. If anything it was central government which proclaimed an open door policy by passing the British Nationality Act of 1948 which declared that any Commonwealth citizen had the right to settle in Britain.

In retrospect the arrival of the *Empire Windrush*

at Tilbury in 1948, carrying 494 Jamaicans to the 'Mother Country', has been fixed on as a defining nexus of change. In reality the process was already a century old. The catastrophic cumulative failure of Ireland's potato harvests in the 1840s provoked the forced migration of perhaps a million Irish, of whom tens of thousands sought survival on the unwelcoming streets of London. The failed liberal revolutions of 1848 brought political refugees like Karl Marx to slum it in squalor in Soho but far larger numbers of Germans followed in his footsteps as economic migrants to become pork butchers, restaurant waiters, musicians and commercial clerks. The foundation of the Blue Funnel line in 1865 and the opening of the Suez Canal in 1869 led to the growth of a 'Chinatown' in Limehouse, which in practice embraced Malays, Burmese and diverse other representatives of the catch-all category of 'lascar'. Sikhs were settling around Gravesend and Bengalis along Brick Lane by the 1920s. Maltese arrived in numbers in the same decade. The pressures underlying these migrations were broadly economic, either the negative push of poverty or the positive pull of opportunity.

While these forces would continue to operate on London throughout the rest of the century, creating communities of Brazilians, Moroccans, Poles and Portuguese purely political factors would add an extra dimension to the process.

The 1930s witnessed the arrival of some fifty thousand émigrés fleeing Fascism in its various manifestations in Spain, Germany and Austria, plus some 10,000 unaccompanied children rescued by the *Kindertransport* rescue scheme of 1938-9.

In the aftermath of World War Two the British government recognised the extraordinary service rendered to the nation by the 130,000 Poles who had served under its flag and, granting right of residence to those who had no wish to return to a devastated homeland under Communist domination, created a unique Resettlement Scheme with a budget of £120,000,000 which was so successful in skills training, language enhancement and job placement that it was wound up ahead of schedule and under budget. Migration from the Subcontinent was hastened by the partition of India and Pakistan in 1947, though the numbers initially involved were small. The uprising by which the former East Pakistan declared its independence as Bangladesh in 1971 led to a far larger migration of Bengalis, most joining the existing community established around Brick Lane, a district which subsequently became officially designated as 'Banglatown'.

China's civil war of 1945-49 ended in a Communist victory which caused thousands to flee southwards from Shanghai and Canton to seek a safe haven in Hong Kong. From there an adventurous minority would press on to settle in Soho, establishing a new Chinatown to replace the old Limehouse settlement which had been blitzed out of existence. Cypriots fleeing the 'emergency' caused by terrorists seeking union with Greece settled in north London from the mid-1950s onwards.

The failure of the anti-Communist Hungarian uprising of 1956 led to the arrival of some twenty thousand refugees. Like those who fled the failure of the 'Prague Spring' of 1968 or the overthrow of the Allende regime in Chile in 1973, this influx, although modest, contained a high proportion of the politically active. Post-independence policies of Africanisation in Kenya and Uganda led in 1967 and 1972 respectively to the expulsion of Asian minorities which had dominated their commerce and professions. They arrived at Heathrow, settled in the surrounding boroughs and prospered. In 1989-92 to ease the pressures they had created as refugees in Hong Kong Britain accepted 'boat people', mostly of Chinese ethnic origin, who had fled Communist Vietnam.

Fresh waves of what became increasingly known as 'asylum-seekers' arrived in the 1990s as a result of wars which caused states to disintegrate in Africa, the Balkans, the Middle East and elsewhere, creating new communities of Kurds, Kashmiris and and Kossovan Albanians, Somalis and Sri Lankans, Afghans and Angolans, Iraqis and Zimbabweans.

Significantly the distribution of London's ethnic minority population is no longer skewed towards the East End or, indeed, to the inner city. London's most important mosque complex is located in Regent's Park. The largest Hindu temple outside India is at Neasden. The borough with the highest proportion of ethnic minority residents is Brent. Ealing, which became the most favoured area of settlement for post-war Poles and also has a significant Somali community, has London's largest populations of Indians, Iraqis and Afghans.

Getting Along

Perhaps the most remarkable outcome of this demographic diversification is the extent to which London's political life has *not* become racialised. Compared with the sort of racially-inspired mass-destruction which was to devastate Los Angeles, Detroit and Chicago in the post-war decades London's negative experiences were to prove minor indeed. The Report of the Commission on Integration and Cohesion published in June 2007 specifically highlighted the extent to which Londoners positively revelled in the rainbow nature of the capital's population. Notwithstanding the headline-grabbing antics of a few high-profile Muslim extremists or the abuse of the hospitality of a democracy represented by the preaching of inflammatory sermons and trafficking in drugs and forged papers at Finsbury Park mosque, the overall picture has been one of political assimilation as members of ethnic minorities have sought election as local councillors or been recruited as employees in Town Halls across the capital. The achievement has, however, been by no means equal between different groups, reflecting striking differences of linguistic assimilation, educational success and commitment to London as a permanent home.

The one glaring exception to this was the ongoing pursuit of an ancient feud. The last public execution to take place in London, outside Newgate prison in 1868, was of Michael Barrett, a Fenian terrorist bomber who, in a bungled attempt to rescue comrades imprisoned in

138. Survivor – St Ethelburga, demolished by an IRA bomb, rebuilt as a Centre for Peace and Reconciliation.

Clerkenwell succeeded only in blowing up a row of houses and killing six innocent people. For six of the ten decades of the twentieth century, even during the blitz, Londoners would be at risk from Irish bombers and gunmen.

In 1979 Airey Neave MP was killed by a bomb secreted under his car in the underground car park of the Palace of Westminster by the Irish National Liberation Army. In 1982 soldiers were the victims of explosive devices placed at Horse Guards and Regent's Park. In 1983 an IRA bomb was exploded outside Harrod's killing six Christmas shoppers and injuring ninety. This was unusual because it risked killing American tourists and the USA remained a significant arena for fund-raising by Irish nationalist front organisations. In 1992 St. Mary Axe was devastated by a lorry bomb, rendering the Baltic Exchange so unsafe that it had to be demolished. A year later Bishopsgate suffered the same fate. Exploded on a Saturday morning when the City was deserted the explosion was intended to destroy property, rather than lives, and halt the operation of the City as a financial market. The property damage ran to hundreds of millions but the City opened for business as usual the following Monday. The fifteenth century church of St. Ethelburga, which had survived the Great Fire and the Blitz only to be reduced to a pile of rubble, was eventually rebuilt as a centre for peace and reconciliation. The last major IRA explosion devastated the Heron Quay/South Quay area of the Isle of Dogs. A breakaway cell of die-hards continued to conduct minor 'operations' in the area of Hammersmith. Throughout these trials Londoners understood perfectly that terrorism was not endorsed by the vast majority of Irish residents who accounted for no less than five per cent of the capital's population. Such hostility as may have been manifested was at an individual rather than a communal level.

In the 1950s it was still perfectly legal for a landlord to put a card in the front window openly stating 'No Irish, No Coloureds'. Denied access to decent accommodation newcomers from the Caribbean were easy victims for unscrupulous and brutal slum landlords like Pyotr Rachman, himself a Polish ex-serviceman. Combining strong-arm intimidation of tenants in parallel with providing rooms for prostitutes, Rachman built a property empire in Notting Hill and Shepherd's Bush and, despite the campaigning efforts of the local MP and newspaper, successfully evaded gaol, died a millionaire and bequeathed his name to the English language as a synonym for exploitation – Rachmanism.

Notting Hill in 1958 achieved an unwanted fame as the setting for what the press called 'race riots' but were in fact a series of individual attacks on West Indian residents by white 'youths' attracted from all over London by the opportunity for gratuitous violence. When the police belatedly acknowledged the situation and enabled magistrates to hand out some stiff sentences for offenders the situation was swiftly calmed. One positive response to the situation was the establishment of an annual Notting Hill carnival which became the largest outdoor gathering in Europe, attracting over a million revellers to the streets of the area on the last weekend of August each year and eventually metamorphosing from its Trinidadian roots to embrace dozens of London's various cultures and counter-cultures. Less happily the tensions of the area attracted the attentions of the revived British Fascist movement in the form of the National Front, which established a local branch in the area. Sir Oswald Mosley returned from self-imposed exile in France to fish in muddied waters but was soundly rejected at the polls.

It was perhaps significant that a re-emergence of support for the Far Right, this time in the shape of the British National Party, was also linked to grievances about the allocation of housing. To the alarm of Labour in May 2006 sufficient councillors were elected to the council of Barking and Dagenham, once a bastion of the white working class, to make them the second largest party.

Evening All ...
If London politics avoided any overt tendency to become fragmented on ethnic or religious lines, London's policing was faced with quite novel challenges in relation to new non-white communities and indigenous Londoners' reactions to them. The cosy, stable Cockney subtopia represented in the long-running television series *Dixon of Dock Green* was being subverted by new demographic realities even as the programmes were being broadcast. Immigrant communities initially too preoccupied by the economics of survival to become politically engaged could be mobilised by perceived failures in policing. For the community which increasingly described itself as Afro-Caribbean or black rather than 'West Indian', defining incidents included the unprovoked racist murder of Kelso Cochrane in 1959, the heavy-handed policing of the Notting Hill carnival in the 1970s and the failure to identify the cause of the fire which claimed the lives of thirteen teenagers at a party in New Cross in 1981. The normally quiescent

Bangladeshi community was similarly politicised by the gratuitous murder of teenage Altab Ali in 1976. The almost incomprehensible police incompetence which botched the investigation of the murder of black teenager Stephen Lawrence in 1993 outraged even the *Daily Mail* and led to the wide-ranging Macpherson Report which accused the Metropolitan Police of "institutional racism" and led to far-reaching changes in its procedures.

Going Global

The technological and institutional revolutions loosely parcelled together under the catch-all label of 'globalisation' have had their reflection in a London which has thereby become an arena for the display and prosecution of political allegiances far remote from its own local concerns. In *Soft City* the travel writer Jonathan Raban observed that whenever there was trouble anywhere in the world sooner or later its reverberations ended up as graffiti along the Earl's Court Road. Stencilled demands for the liberation of the leader of the Peruvian Marxist terrorist movement Sendero Luminoso ('Shining Path') once regularly adorned the elegantly stuccoed streets of Notting Hill. In 1968 violent protests outside the US Embassy in Grosvenor Square against the American war in Vietnam were watched on television by the bemused residents of London's leafy suburbs.

As the Cold War intensified with the advent of the hydrogen bomb and advances in missile capability London became the focus for an institutionalised protest against British possession of nuclear weapons. Founded in 1958 the Campaign for Nuclear Disarmament attracted the prominent support of intellectuals such as Michael Foot, J.B. Priestley and Bertrand Russell, who served as its first President and courted arrest by high-profile non-violent acts of civil disobedience. By the early 1960s crowds of up to 150,000 were attracted to the London rally which ended its annual Easter trek from the Atomic Weapons Research Establishment at Aldermaston in Berkshire. The 1963 Nuclear Test Ban Treaty led to a diminution in mass-

support but the deployment of American Cruise missiles in the UK after 1979 led to a revival which died back again with the ending of the Cold War in the 1990s.

A similar trajectory was followed by another single-issue institutionalised campaign. In 1959 Trevor Huddleston, an austere Anglican incarnation of the quintessential turbulent priest, launched a campaign to boycott South African goods in protest against its government's apartheid system of racial oppression. In 1960 this initiative hardened into the Anti-Apartheid Movement, which became the largest such organisation apart from South Africa's own internal liberation movements. The AAM extended the concept of the boycott to disinvestments and the imposition of economic, cultural and sporting sanctions. Mass demonstrations harassed the Springbok rugby tour of 1969-70 and led to the cancellation of the cricket tour scheduled for the following season. The visit of South African Prime Minister P.W. Botha to London in 1984 was met by a protest demonstration 50,000 strong. In 1985 Huddleston led a 100,000-strong march through the capital. In 1986 London-based Barclays Bank finally closed down its South African operations, explicitly acknowledging the pressure exerted by the AAM. In 1988 to mark the seventieth birthday of the imprisoned African National Congress leader Nelson Mandela, the AAM organised a huge concert at Wembley Stadium, attracting a crowd of 80,000.

For over a decade a twenty-four-hour vigil on Mandela's behalf was maintained on the pavement outside South Africa House. Following the holding of democratic elections in South Africa in 1994 the Anti-Apartheid Movement was dissolved that year.

Domestic issues could still provoke mass-demonstrations like the violent anti-poll tax riots of 1990, which left three hundred injured and led to as many arrests. The Countryside Alliance march of 2002 against the ban on fox-hunting and other alleged threats to rural livelihoods and lifestyles claimed to be the largest ever seen in London, attracting 400,000 participants. But

139. Crying in the Wilderness? – Demonstrators against the 1982 Falklands War pass through an empty City of London.

it was the threat of mass-starvation in distant Ethiopia which inspired the huge Live Aid concert in 1984 and its reprise twenty years later. And the scale of the Countryside Alliance protest was matched, if not surpassed, by the marches against the Iraq wars of 1991 and 2003. Organisers of the 2003 march claimed that two million had taken part; even the police conceded a figure of 750,000.

The Royals

Dismissed at the dinner-tables of Hampstead and Islington as a distraction from 'real' politics, the monarchy has not only survived into the twenty-first century but has also occasioned public displays of allegiance which have confounded both critics and sceptics. Londoners may no longer have stood at respectful attention for the National Anthem at the end of an evening at the cinema or the theatre but they still thronged the streets for a royal.

It was the future Queen Mother, rather than the dutiful but reserved King, who won the hearts of Londoners with her tireless tours of bombed areas during the blitz, establishing a 'special relationship' which was to sustain her self-reinvention as 'the Queen Mum' after the early death of the careworn George VI. The enthusiasm which attended the celebration of her hundredth birthday in the year of the Millennium and the affectionate reverence which motivated hundreds of thousands to make their personal farewells during her lying-in-state in Westminster Hall testified to her appeal to succeeding generations.

The coronation of Queen Elizabeth II in 1953 was the first to be televised and itself is claimed to have prompted the sale of half a million television sets. Over the succeeding half century the House of Windsor would have no option but to evolve into a Media Monarchy. The Queen's Christmas Broadcast established itself as part of the rituals of the festive season and eventually the Queen herself appeared to become a more relaxed broadcaster. Deference died by decades. The guying of the monarchy, along with other traditional institutions, began with the advent of 'satire' on stage and screen in the early 1960s. Compared with the no-holds-barred jeering puppets of *Spitting Image* two decades later, it was mild stuff.

With the marriage of the Prince of Wales to Lady Diana Spencer at St. Paul's cathedral in 1981 before a global television audience of a billion the House of Windsor acquired a fairy princess who turned into a global media superstar, guaranteed to raise the sales of any publication 10% by simply appearing on its cover. The camera – newspaper, television or film – loved her as it loved no other royal. Her death and funeral in 1997 provoked an outburst of unprecedented displays of public grief outside Kensington Palace and Westminster Abbey, prompting a serious debate about what sort of people the British had become. The Queen's decision to retreat with her bereaved grandsons to privacy in Scotland and the omission to fly the royal standard over Buckingham Palace at half mast were interpreted with hostility by Diana's partisans as gestures of cold-heartedness and disrespect. The widespread tabloid opinion that the sovereign ought to be in London at a time of national mourning was peculiarly revealing of the capital's place in the national psyche. Nine years later the story of that week was immortalised as a film simply entitled *The Queen*.

Five years after the death of Diana anti-monarchists predicted that the sovereign's forthcoming Golden Jubilee would be a flop. A million people filled the Mall to prove them wrong.

Eastward Ho!

If Professor Abercrombie's wartime plans for restructuring London went largely unrealised post-war London changed mightily all the same. Conservative governments relaxed most controls on building in the 1950s, initiating a construction boom which littered the city with a great deal of rather inferior commercial architecture. The tower-block became the icon of the decade. Croydon embraced it to commence the creation of a virtual satellite city of office skyscrapers. Newham saw it as the quick-fix solution to the post-war housing shortage – bulldoze the slums away and stand the streets up in the sky sideways. The collapse of five floors of Ronan Point in 1968 following a gas explosion revealed major structural failings which prompted a re-think, though not before Erno Goldfinger's Trellick Tower marked a final, defiant profession of faith in the concept of the vertical neighbourhood.

The wanton demolition of the Euston Arch in 1962 sounded a clarion call to halt the heedless demolition of London's built heritage in pursuit of profit and supposed progress. Civic societies proliferated in defence of the vestigial historic remains of the capital's various 'villages'. From 1968 onwards not just individual buildings or streets but whole neighbourhoods could be protected from the wrecking-ball by designation as a 'conservation area'. Plans to raze Soho and revamp Covent Garden were soundly defeated. The decayed Docklands offered more of a blank canvas for the developers and their mini-Manhattan frightened the City into rebuilding a third of its office space in a decade and a half. Other counter-currents to the *Drang Nach Osten* included major projects to reclaim the industrial wasteland north of King's Cross and to fill in the canal basin at Paddington.

The attempt to sustain the momentum in the east by making the Millennium Dome a focal point for further investment proved a costly fiasco, although its construction did entail the extension of the Jubilee Line from Westminster to Stratford. In the event this proved to be a useful component in establishing the feasibility of making Stratford and the surrounding Lea Valley area the optimal location for hosting the Olympic Games of 2012. Prime Minister Tony Blair and London Mayor Ken Livingstone set aside their differences to present a convincing case to the International Olympic Committee at Singapore, clinching the London presentation by importing a platoon of Stratford schoolchildren representative of all five continents, indisputable living proof of London's standing – World City.

Chronology

60-61 Boudiccan revolt
ca. 65 Death of Classicianus
122 Emperor Hadrian visits Londinium
193 Revolt of Clodius Albinus
286 Revolt of Carausius
410 Emperor Honorius confirms withdrawal of Roman legions
604 Foundation of St. Paul's
842, 851 Major Viking raids
871-72 Vikings winter in London
886 Alfred the Great orders the reoccupation and refortification of London
1032 Court of Husting known to exist
1066 William I is crowned in Westminster Abbey (December 25th)
1067 William I confirms rights of Londoners
1097-99 Westminster Hall built
1101 First use of the Tower of London as a political prison
ca. 1132 Henry I grants Londoners the right to elect their own sheriffs
1141 Londoners prevent coronation of Queen Matilda
1189 First mention of the office of (Lord) Mayor
1215 King John confirms the right of Londoners to elect their Mayor. Mayor of London included in guarantors of Magna Carta
1237 First record of granting the Freedom of the City
1283 First record of the term Lord Mayor
1285 Crown takes over administration of the City of London
First meeting of ward representatives, forerunner of Common Council
1290 Edward I expels Jewish community
1295 Model Parliament
1305 Execution of William Wallace at Smithfield
1308 First use of Coronation chair
1348 Order of the Garter established
1349 Black Death
1381 Peasants' Revolt
1382 Liber Regalis records order of coronation service
1384 Regular elections begin for Court of Common Council
1394-1401 Major alterations to Westminster Hall
1411-40 Guildhall built
1419 John Croxton compiles Liber Albus
1422 First Mayoral procession by water
1450 Jack Cade's rebellion

1471 Murder of Henry VI in Wakefield Tower
1476 William Caxton establishes first printing press at Westminster
1483 Murder of Edward V in the Tower
1484 College of Arms founded to regulate heraldry
1497 Cornish rebels defeated at Blackheath
1498 Henry VII builds royal palace at Richmond
1501 First Lord Mayor's Banquet held in Guildhall
1509 St. Paul's School founded
1514 Court of Aldermen establishes precedence of Livery Companies
Trinity House established
1515-20 Bridewell Palace built
1516 Thomas More Utopia
1517 Evil May Day riots victimise Flemish minority
1518 Henry VIII charters College of Physicians
1526 Cardinal Wolsey presents Hampton Court to Henry VIII
1529 Henry VIII confiscates York Place to become the Palace of Whitehall
1531 Henry VIII seizes St. James's Hospital
1534 Henry VIII secures royal supremacy over the church in England
1535 Execution of Sir Thomas More
1536-40 Suppression of religious houses
1537 Honourable Artillery Company founded
1538 Parish registration of baptisms, marriages and funerals
1539 Distribution of a royally sanctioned English Bible
1540 Execution of Thomas Cromwell at Tower Hill
1548 Edward VI issues first English prayer book
1550 First settlement of French Huguenots
1553 Execution of Lady Jane Grey
1554 Sir Thomas Wyatt's rebellion
1555 John Rogers burned at Smithfield
1558 Elizabeth I proclaims herself Supreme Governor of the Church of England
1570 Excommunication of Elizabeth I
1571 Royal Exchange opened
1588 Celebration of Armada's defeat in St. Paul's Cathedral
1605 Gunpowder Plot foiled
First Stuart court masque performed
1613 Foundation of the Irish Society
1614 St. Margaret's Westminster adopted as parish church of the House of Commons
1622 Completion of the Banqueting House
1627 Francis Bacon New Atlantis
1641 Execution of the Earl of Strafford

	Puritans gain control of Common Council
1642	4th January Charles I attempts the arrest of 5 MPs
	13th November royalist forces turned back from Turnham Green
1642	(October) - 1643 (May) fortification of London
1643	Demolition of Paul's Cross
1644	Globe Theatre and Strand maypole demolished
	John Milton *Areopagitica*
1645	Execution of Archbishop Laud at Tower Hill
1647	Putney Debates
1648	Abortive royalist rising
1649	Trial and execution of Charles I (January 30th)
1651	Thomas Hobbes *Leviathan*
1652	Churches ordered closed on Christmas Day
	Hyde Park sold
	First coffee-house opened
1656	Readmission of Jewish community
1658	State funeral of Oliver Cromwell
1660	Restoration of Charles II (May 29th)
1662	Licensing Act restores censorship over printing
1665	Great Plague forces evacuation of royal court
1666	Great Fire of London
1675	Attempted royal suppression of coffee-houses
1685	Revocation of the Edict of Nantes provokes Huguenot immigration
	Execution of the Duke of Monmouth at Tower Hill
1689	John Locke *Two Treatises on Government*
	Bill of Rights
1694	Foundation of the Bank of England
1695	Licensing Act allowed to lapse
1698	Whitehall Palace destroyed by fire
	Foundation of the Society for the Promotion of Christian Knowledge
1701	Act of Settlement regulates succession to the throne
1702	*Daily Courant*, London's first daily newspaper, begins publication
1707	Act of Union merges parliaments of England and Scotland
1711	Fifty New Churches Act
1717	George I ceases to attend meetings of the Cabinet
1720	South Sea Bubble
1725	George I revives the Order of the Bath
1727	Handel's *Zadok the Priest* coronation anthem
1733	Walpole's Excise Bill withdrawn
1734	Voltaire *Lettres Philosophiques*
1735	Beef-Steak Society founded
	10 Downing Street becomes the official residence of the First Lord of the Treasury
1739-52	Mansion House built
1745	Thomas Arne *God Bless Great George Our King*
1750	Board of Deputies established by Jewish community leaders
1753	Jewish Naturalization Act
1762	Westminster Paving Act
1763	No. 45 *The North Briton*
1768	John Wilkes elected MP for Middlesex
1770	Lord Mayor Beckford reproves George III
1772	Lord Mansfield rules slavery illegal in Britain

	in Somersett case
1776	Adam Smith *An Enquiry into the Causes of the Wealth of Nations*
	John Cartwright *Take Your Choice*
	Jeremy Bentham *A Fragment on Government*
1780	Gordon riots
1781	Society for Constitutional Information established
1785	*The Times* first published as the *Daily Universal Register*
1788	George III suffers period of derangement
1790	Edmund Burke *Reflections on the Revolution in France*
1791	Tom Paine *The Rights of Man*
1792	London Corresponding Society established
	Outbreak of war with France
	Mary Wollstonecraft *A Vindication of the Rights of Women*
1793	William Godwin *Enquiry Concerning Political Justice*
1794	Horne Tooke acquitted of treason
1799	Viscardo Y Guzman *Letter to the Spanish Americans*
1801	First census
1802	Cobbett's *Political Register* begins publication
1806	Funeral of Lord Nelson
1809	Imprisonment of Sir Francis Burdett
1811	Prince of Wales becomes Regent
1812	Assassination of Spencer Perceval in the House of Commons
	First Hampden Club founded
1816	Spa Fields Riot
1817	Prince of Wales' coach stoned in the Mall
	Habeas Corpus suspended
1820	Caroline of Brunswick attempts to claim her right to the throne
	Cato Street Conspiracy
1828	No. 11 Downing Street becomes official residence of the Chancellor of the Exchquer
1829	Metropolitan Police established
	Roman Catholic Emancipation
1832	First Reform Act
1834	Houses of Parliament burned down
1836	Reform Club founded
1838	People's Charter drawn up
1848	Last major Chartist demonstration
1851	Great Exhibition
1852	Funeral of the Duke of Wellington
1854-56	Crimean War
1855	Establishment of the Metropolitan Board of Works
	Daily Telegraph first published
	Hyde Park demonstration against Sunday Trading Bill
1856	Last Mayoral procession on the Thames
	Victoria Cross instituted
1857	Indian Army mutiny
1858	Lionel de Rothschild elected M.P. for the City of London
1859	John Stuart Mill *On Liberty*
1864	Garibaldi feted in London
1866-7	Reform riots at Hyde Park

1867	Second Reform Act enfranchises the urban working man
1868	Last public execution. Michael Barrett, Fenian bomber, outside Newgate
	Foundation of Trades Union Congress
1869	J.S. Mill *The Subjection of Women*
1871	Paris Communards flee to London
1872	Speaker's Corner sanctioned by statute
	Albert Memorial completed
1881	Special Branch established
	International Anarchist Congress held in London
1882	Press Club founded
	National Liberal Club founded
	Law Courts moved to Strand
1884	Fabian Society founded
1885	Fenians bomb Westminster Hall
1886	Charles Bradlaugh sworn in as a Member of Parliament by affirmation
1887	Queen Victoria's Golden Jubilee
	'Bloody Sunday' riot in Trafalgar Square
1888	*Financial Times* established
	Match Girls' Strike
1889	Establishment of the London County Council
	Dock strike
	Fabian Essays on Socialism
1891	William Morris *News from Nowhere*
1892	Dadobhai Naoroji elected as Britain's first non-white MP
1893	Independent Labour Party founded
1894	Local Government Act grants the vote to some women at local elections
1895	London School of Economics founded
1896	*Daily Mail* first published
1896	Royal Victorian Order established
1897	Queen Victoria's Diamond Jubilee
1899	Establishment of 28 Metropolitan Boroughs
	Statue of Oliver Cromwell unveiled
1900	*Daily Express* first published
	Pan-African Congress meets in London
	Labour Party founded as the Labour Representation Committee
1901	Funeral of Queen Victoria
1903	*Daily Mirror* first published
1904	London School Board functions absorbed by LCC
1905	Aliens Act imposes immigration controls
1906	Women's Social and Political Union moves to London
1907	Progressives lose control of LCC in landslide election
	'Women's Parliament' at Caxton Hall
1908	Anglo-French exhibition at White City
	London hosts Olympic Games
	Suffragettes chain themselves to the railings of No.10 Downing Street
1909	Secret Service bureau established
1910	London Labour Party established
	Victoria Memorial unveiled
1911	Siege of Sidney Street
1912	*Daily Herald* first published
1913	Battersea chooses John Archer as Britain's first black Mayor
	Funeral of Suffragette 'martyr' Emily Davison
1914	Expulsion of German and Austrian nationals
	Arrival of Belgian refugees
1917	London bombed by German Gotha bombers
1920	Cenotaph unveiled at funeral of the Unknown Warrior
	Communist Party of Great Britain founded
	Imperial War Museum opened
1921	British Legion founded
	Poplar Council rates revolt
1922	British Broadcasting Company founded
	County Hall opened
	Conservative backbench 1922 Committee established at Carlton Club meeting
	First 'Hunger March'
1924-25	British Empire Exhibition at Wembley
1926	General Strike
	British Broadcasting Corporation established
1930	*Daily Worker* first published
	Statue of Mrs. Emmeline Pankhurst unveiled
1931	Dr. Harold Moody founds the League of Coloured Peoples
1932	George V makes first Christmas broadcast
	British Union of Fascists founded
1933	Marx Memorial Library established
	London Passenger Transport Board established
1934	Labour achieves control of L.C.C.
1935	Jubilee of King George V
1936	Abdication crisis
	'Battle of Cable Street'
	Trial television broadcasting begins
	Peace Pledge Union founded
	Left Book Club founded
	'Jarrow Crusade'
1937	Coronation of King George VI, first to be filmed
	British Institute of Public Opinion founded
	Mass Observation founded
	Air Raid Precautions Act
1938	London and Home Counties Act establishes Green Belt
1939	Mass evacuation of London
1940	(September 7th)-1941(May 10th) London endures Luftwaffe blitz
	Home Guard established
1941	Last prisoner executed in the Tower of London
1942	Beveridge Report published
1944	(June 13th) – 1945 (March 27th) V-weapons launched against London
1945	May 8th V.E. Day
	Labour landslide general election victory
	August 15th V.J. DAy
1946	(8th June) Victory Day parade
	Inaugural session of UN General Assembly at Methodist Hall, Westminster
	Bank of England nationalised
	Resumption of TV broadcasting
	Arts Council established
1947	Partition of India and Pakistan
	Polish Resettlement Act
1948	London hosts Olympic Games
	Wedding of Princess Elizabeth and Lt. Philip Mountbatten

CHRONOLOGY

National Health Service established
Empire Windrush docks at Tilbury
British Nationality Act
1949 George Orwell *1984*
Passport to Pimlico
Clothes rationing ends
1950 Petrol rationing ends
Re-opening of restored House of Commons
Stone of Scone stolen from coronation chair in Westminster Abbey
1951 Festival of Britain
Intelligence agents Guy Burgess and Donald Maclean defect to USSR
1952 Death of George VI
Identity cards abolished
1953 Coronation of Elizabeth II, first to be televised
1954 Rationing ends
1955 Inauguration of commercial television
1956 Trafalgar Square demonstration against Suez Canal intervention
Arrival of refugees from failed Hungarian uprising
1957 Royal Commission on the Government of London
National Opinion Polls (N.O.P.) founded
1958 Campaign for Nuclear Disarmament founded
Notting Hill 'race riots'
Last presentation of debutantes at court
1959 *Manchester Guardian* relocates to London
State Opening of Parliament first televised
Murder of Kelso Cochrane
1960 Anti-Apartheid Movement founded
1960-64 Major refurbishment of 10 Downing Street
1961 *Beyond the Fringe*
1962 Commonwealth Immigration restricts entry to Britain
Demolition of Euston Arch
1963 Profumo scandal
That Was The Week That Was
1964 First Notting Hill carnival
C.P. Snow *The Corridors of Power*
1965 London County Council replaced by the Greater London Council
State funeral of Sir Winston Churchill
1967 Arrival of Asian passport-holders expelled from Kenya
Conservatives take control of G.L.C.
1968 Mass demonstrations against Vietnam war
Arrival of Czechoslovak refugees from failure of the 'Prague Spring'
1969 Students. protests close London School of Economics
1971 UK joins European Economic Community
Decimalisation of currency
Angry Brigade bombing campaign
1972 Arrival of Asian passport holders expelled from Uganda
1976 Murder of Altab Ali
Commission for Racial Equality established
1977 Silver Jubilee of Queen Elizabeth II – 4,000 London street parties

1978 House of Commons debates broadcast by radio
'Winter of Discontent' – widespread strike disruption of public services
1979 Airey Neave MP killed by INLA bomb in the Palace of Westminster
1980 Iranian Embassy siege
Riots in Deptford and Southall
1981 Wedding of Prince Charles and Lady Diana Spencer
Riots in Brixton
Social Democrat Party established by 'Gang of Four'
London Docklands Development Corporation established
British Nationality Act
1982 British National Party founded
IRA bomb Horse Guards and Regent's Park, killing ten
1983 IRA bomb explodes outside Harrod's killing 6
1984 Live Aid concert for famine relief in Africa
Murder of PC Yvonne Fletcher in front of Libyan Embassy
1985 Riots in Brixton and Tottenham
House of Lords debates first televised
1986 Abolition of the Greater London Council
The Independent first published
'Big Bang' deregulation of City of London financial markets
1988 Charter '88 founded
SDP merges with Liberal Party to form Liberal Democrats
1989 First live television broadcast from the House of Commons
1990 Violent anti poll-tax riots in Trafalgar Square
1991 IRA mortar attack on 10 Downing Street
Mass demonstration against Iraq war
1992 St. Mary Axe devastated by IRA bomb
1993 Bishopsgate devastated by IRA bomb
Murder of Stephen Lawrence
1994 Anti-Apartheid Movement dissolved
1995 Communist Party of Great Britain dissolved
1997 Funeral of Diana, Princess of Wales
1999 Macpherson Report accuses Metropolitan Police of 'institutional racism'
2000 Ken Livingstone becomes first elected Mayor of London
Millennium Dome
Pope John Paul II nominates St. Thomas More as patron saint of politicians
2001 Portcullis House opened
2002 Golden Jubilee of Queen Elizabeth II
Mass demonstration by Countryside Alliance
2003 Mass demonstration against Iraq war
2004 Ken Livingstone re-elected Mayor
2005 Muslim suicide bombers kill 52 in rush-hour attacks on transport passengers
2007 Statue of Nelson Mandela unveiled in Parliament Square
2012 London scheduled to host Olympic Games

Reading List

D. Ascoli: *The Queen's Peace : The Origins and Development of the Metropolitan Police 1829-1979* (Hamish Hamilton 1979)

R. Ashton: *The City and the Court 1603-43* (Cambridge University Press 1979)

J. Blackwood: *London's Immortals : The Complete Outdoor Commemorative Statues* (Savoy Press 1989)

C. Bloom: *Violent London: 2000 Years of Riots, Rebels and Revolts* (Sidgwick & Jackson 2003)

S. Bradley and N. Pevsner: *The Buildings of England London 1: The City of London* (Yale U.P. 2002) 6: *Westminster* (Yale U.P. 2003)

S. Brigden: *London and the Reformation* (Oxford University Press 1989)

C. Brooke and G. Keir: *London 800-1216 : the shaping of a city* (Secker and Warburg 1975)

J. Davis: *Reforming London : the London Government Problem 1855-1900* (Clarendon Press 1988)

G. Dench, K. Gavron, M. Young: *The New East End : Kinship, Race and Conflict* (Profile Books 2006)

B. Donoughue, G.W. Jones, P. Mandelson: *Herbert Morrison. Portrait of a Politician* (Weidenfeld & Nicolson 2001)

F. Driver and D. Gilbert: *Imperial Cities : Landscape, Display and Identity* (Manchester University Press 1999)

F.F. Foster: *The Politics of Stability : A Portrait of the Rulers in Elizabethan London* (Royal Historical Society 1977)

P.K. Gilbert (ed.): *Imagined Londons* (State University of New York Press 2002)

D. Goodway: *London Chartism 1838-48* (Cambridge University Press 1982)

A. Goodwin: *The Friends of Liberty : the English Democratic Movement in the Age of the French Revolution* (Harvard University Press 1979)

T. Harris: *London Crowds in the Reign of Charles II: Politics and Propaganda from the Restoration until the Exclusion Crisis* (Cambridge University Press 1987)

S. Inwood: *A History of London* (Macmillan 1998)

W.E. Jackson: *Achievement : A Short History of the London County Council* (Longmans 1965)

K. Livingstone: *If Voting Changed Anything, They'd Abolish It* (HarperCollins 1987)

F. MacCarthy: *William Morris : A Life for Our Time* (Faber & Faber 1994)

J. Marriott: *The Culture of Labourism : the East End Between the Wars* (Edinburgh U.P. 1991)

T. McCarthy: *The Great Dock Strike 1889* (Weidenfeld & Nicolson 1988)

J. Morris: *Londinium : London in the Roman Empire* (Weidenfeld & Nicolson 1999)

B. Pimlott and N. Rao: *Governing London* (Oxford U.P. 2002)

D. Owen: *The Government of Victorian London 1855-1889:The Metropolitan Board of Works, the Vestries and the City Corporation* (Harvard University Press 1982)

G. Rhodes: *The Government of London : The Struggle for Reform* (University of Toronto Press 1970)

G. Rosser: *Medieval Westminster 1200-1540* (Oxford University Press 2001)

A. Saint (ed): *Politics and the People of London : the London County Council 1889-1965* (Hambledon Press 1989)

W. Sansom: *The Blitz : Westminster at War* (Oxford University Press 1990)

J.B. Seatrobe: *Political London : A Guide to the Capital's Political Sights* (Politico's 2000)

J. Shepherd: *George Lansbury : At the Heart of Old Labour* (Oxford U.P. 2002)

F.H.W. Sheppard: *Local Government in St. Marylebone 1688-1835 : A Study of the Vestry and the Turnpike Trust* (Athlone Press 1958)

D.L. Smith, R. Strier, D. Bevington (eds.): *The Theatrical City : Culture, Theatre and Politics in London 1576-1649* (Cambridge University Press 1995)

R. Strong: *Coronation : From the 8th to the 21st Century* (Trafalgar Square 2007)

R. Tames: *The Westminster and Pimlico Book* (Historical Publications 2005)

P. R. Thompson: *Socialists, Liberals and Labour : the struggle for London 1885-1914* (Routledge & Kegan Paul 1967)

I. Watson: *Westminster and Pimlico Past* (Historical Publications 1993)

G.A. Williams: *Medieval London : From Commune to Capital* (Athlone Press 1963)

P. Wright: *The Strange History of Buckingham Palace* (Sutton 1996)

K. Young, P. Garside: *Metropolitan London : Politics and Urban Change 1837-1981* (Edward Arnold 1982)

P. Ziegler: *London at War 1939-45* (Sinclair-Stevenson 1995)

INDEX
Asterisks denote illustration or caption